EXECUTIVE OFFICE OF THE PRESIDENT
OFFICE OF MANAGEMENT AND BUDGET
WASHINGTON, D.C. 20503

February 27, 2015

The Honorable Ronald Johnson
Chairman
Committee on Homeland Security
  and Governmental Affairs
United States Senate
Washington, D.C. 20510

Dear Mr. Chairman:

The attached report is submitted pursuant to Title III of the E-Government Act of 2002 (P.L. 107-347), which requires the Office of Management and Budget (OMB) to submit an annual report to Congress on implementation by Federal agencies of the Federal Information Security Management Act of 2002 (FISMA). This report covers the period from October 1, 2013, through September 30, 2014, and provides an update of ongoing information security initiatives, a review of Fiscal Year 2014 information security incidents, Inspector General assessments of agencies' progress in implementing information security capabilities, and the Federal Government's progress in meeting key information security performance measures based on agency submitted data. As you will note, progress has been made in key areas of information security.

With the passage of the Federal Information Security Modernization Act of 2014, OMB and the requirements of FISMA were greatly aided in its continued work with agencies to fulfill the requirements of increasingly resilient information technology security and privacy management programs. The new law includes additional requirements to be included in the OMB annual FISMA report to Congress. Given that this law was not signed until December 18, 2014, these new requirements will be addressable in the OMB FISMA report covering FY 2015.

After the conclusion of FY 2014, these new requirements will be addressable in the OMB FISMA report covering FY 2015.

We appreciate the assistance of Congress in supporting these programs, and we look forward to continuing our work on this critical issue. Please contact Tamara Fucile, Associate Director for Legislative Affairs, at (202) 395-4790 if you have any questions.

Sincerely,

Shaun Donovan
Director

Enclosure

Identical Letter Sent to:

The Honorable Thomas R. Carper
The Honorable Jason Chaffetz
The Honorable Elijah Cummings
The Honorable Gene L. Dodaro
The Honorable Eddie Bernice Johnson
The Honorable Michael McCaul
The Honorable Bill Nelson
The Honorable Lamar Smith
The Honorable Bennie G. Thompson
The Honorable John Thune

TABLE OF CONTENTS

INTRODUCTION: FEDERAL CYBERSECURITY YEAR IN REVIEW

As cyber threats continue to evolve, the Federal Government is embarking on a number of initiatives to protect Federal information and assets and improve the resilience of Federal networks. OMB, in coordination with its partners at the National Security Council (NSC), the Department of Homeland Security (DHS), and other agencies, helps drive these efforts in its role overseeing the implementation of programs to combat cyber vulnerabilities and threats to Federal systems. Today, as required by the Federal Information Security Management Act of 2002 (FISMA), OMB is sending to Congress the annual report that tracks the progress of our efforts while also identifying areas of needed improvement.

Agencies take a number of actions to protect government networks and information, implementing tools and policies in order to mitigate potential risks. The fiscal year (FY) 2014 FISMA report provides metrics on Federal cybersecurity incidents, the efforts being undertaken to mitigate them and prevent future incidents, and agency progress in implementing cybersecurity policies and programs to protect their networks. FY 2014 proved to be a year of continued progress toward the Administration's Cybersecurity Cross Agency Priority (CAP) Goal, which requires agencies to "Know Your Network" (Information Security Continuous Monitoring), "Know Your Users" (Strong Authentication), and "Know Your Traffic" (Trusted Internet Connection Consolidation and Capabilities).

- *Know Your Network* – Agency performance implementing Information Security Continuous Monitoring (ISCM) improved from 81% in FY 2013 to 92% in FY 2014. This means that agencies have improved implementation of Asset, Configuration, and Vulnerability Management tools and practices to better manage cyber vulnerabilities when they arise.

- *Know Your Users* – Implementation of Strong Authentication has seen a total increase from 67% in FY 2013 to 72% in FY 2014. This means that an increasing number of agencies require their users to log-on to networks with unique Personal Identity Verification (PIV) cards, instead of other less secure means of identification and authentication.

- *Know Your Traffic* – Agencies achieved the CAP goal of 95% of external network traffic passing through a TIC or Managed Trusted Internet Protocol Services (MTIPS) provider, and implementation of TIC 2.0 capabilities rose from 87% in FY 2013 to 92% in FY 2014. This means that an increasing amount of agency internet traffic passes through trusted internet connections and that agencies are deploying common controls to improve cybersecurity.

Additionally, DHS has continued implementation of key vulnerability and threat prevention initiatives. Under the Continuous Diagnostics and Mitigation (CDM) program, agencies have procured over 1.7 million licenses for asset, configuration, and vulnerability management tools. The President's FY 2016 Budget also invests $582 million to drive continued progress through CDM and EINSTEIN to enable agencies to detect and prevent evolving cyber threats. Moreover, EINSTEIN, an intrusion detection and prevention system, is being deployed to provide agencies with an early warning system, and improved situational awareness of emerging threats.

We have seen notable progress by Federal agencies, but there is work to be done. Fiscal Year 2014, in particular, was a pivotal year for Federal cybersecurity, marked by sophisticated threat activity and vulnerabilities. Federal agencies reported nearly 70,000 information security incidents in FY 2014, up 15% from FY 2013. Strong Authentication remains a key challenge. Although overall Strong Authentication implementation reached 72% in FY 2014, this number is partially buoyed by the size and strong performance of the Department of Defense (DOD). When removing DOD from the calculation, only 41% of civilian CFO Act agencies implemented the use of Strong Authentication for network access in FY 2014. Yet still, agencies are demonstrating a commitment (and even significant progress) to improving in this area. The Department of Commerce (Commerce) saw a dramatic increase in the use of Strong Authentication from 30% to 88% as compared to FY 2013, while the Environmental Protection Agency (EPA) jumped from 0% to 69%.

And we are already taking steps to ensure every CFO Act agency implements Administration priorities to advance the overall state of cybersecurity. For example, last fall OMB issued guidance establishing a new process for DHS to conduct regular and proactive scans of Federal civilian agency networks to enable faster and more comprehensive responses to major cybersecurity vulnerabilities and incidents. We will be able to gauge the progress of this measure in the annual FY 2015 FISMA report. OMB also launched a dedicated cybersecurity unit within the Office of E-Government & Information Technology (E-Gov Cyber) to drive accelerated agency adoption of Administration priorities through:

- o Data-driven, risk-based oversight of agency and government-wide cybersecurity programs;
- o Issuance and implementation of Federal cybersecurity policies consistent with emerging technologies and evolving cyber threats;
- o Oversight and coordination of the Federal response to major cyber incidents and vulnerabilities to ensure appropriate mitigation strategies are implemented effectively; and,
- o Coordination and engagement with NSC staff, DHS, the National Institute of Standards and Technology (NIST), Congress, and other key stakeholders to modernize and implement relevant cybersecurity statutes.

In FY 2015, OMB E-Gov Cyber will drive accelerated agency adoption of Administration priorities and industry best practices as a means of improving the Federal cybersecurity posture.

These and other initiatives are described in detail throughout this report, which covers the period from October 1, 2013, to September 30, 2014. The report is organized as follows:

Section I: Strengthening Federal Cybersecurity

Describes the efforts undertaken to protect existing and emerging government data and information technology (IT) assets and the role OMB plays in Federal cybersecurity efforts.

Section II: State of Federal Cybersecurity

Identifies agency performance against cybersecurity metrics and OMB's assessment of that performance.

Section III: Summary of Inspectors General's Findings

Provides an overview of the assessments of agency inspectors general (IG) regarding agency information security programs.

Section IV: Progress in Meeting Key Privacy Performance Measures

Provides an overview of the agency progress made in implementing steps to analyze and address privacy issues.

Section V: Appendices

Appendix 1: NIST Performance in 2014

SECTION I: STRENGTHENING FEDERAL CYBERSECURITY

The Federal Government is currently facing an evolving cybersecurity landscape. According to data reported to US-CERT, and described in more detail in Section II, Phishing and Malicious Code continue to present threats to both the Federal Government and public at large. These increasingly sophisticated attacks take advantage of flaws in software code or use exploits that can circumvent signature-based tools that commonly identify and prevent known threats. Far too often, adversaries are able to employ social engineering techniques designed to trick the unsuspecting user to open a malicious link or attachment thereby giving the attacker direct access to Federal information and information systems. The following section describes how the Federal Government is addressing these and other cyber threats.

A. FEDERAL GOVERNMENT PROGRAMS DESIGNED TO COMBAT GROWING THREATS

The Federal Government relies on a variety of initiatives to ensure the continued protection of Federal information and information systems. First, FISMA requires agencies to maintain an information security program commensurate with their risk profile. For instance, agencies are responsible for assessing and authorizing information systems to operate within their own networks and for determining what users have the authority to access agency information. Second, DHS is the operational lead for Federal civilian cybersecurity, and as such, executes a number of protection programs on behalf of the Government. Third, NIST issues and updates security standards and guidelines for information systems utilized by Federal agencies. Finally, OMB, in partnership with NSC staff and DHS, oversees the successful implementation of agency-specific and government-wide cybersecurity programs.

OMB's oversight efforts focus, among other evaluation criteria, on measuring agency performance against the Cybersecurity CAP Goal. As described in more detail in Section II, the Cybersecurity CAP Goal was designed to assess agency implementation of basic cybersecurity principles to ensure a common Federal baseline for combating cyber threats. Section II of this report describes the performance of agency-specific cybersecurity programs, including those that fall under both the CAP goal and key FISMA metrics. The remainder of this section highlights select government-wide cybersecurity programs and OMB's role in Federal cybersecurity. It is important to note that the following programs are some of the most critical, but do not represent the universe of Federal cybersecurity initiatives.

Government-wide Programs Administered by DHS

As described above, DHS is the operational lead for Federal civilian cybersecurity and is responsible for deploying key programs that, when fully implemented, will provide agencies with strong protection against emerging threats. The two most critical programs are:

- Continuous Diagnostics & Mitigation; and

- National Cybersecurity Protection System (EINSTEIN).

Continuous Diagnostics & Mitigation

Per *OMB Memorandum 14-03, "Ensuring the Security of Federal Information and Information Systems,"* DHS, in partnership with OMB and NSC staff, operates the *Continuous Diagnostics & Mitigation (CDM)* program. Under CDM, DHS works with the General Services Administration (GSA) to establish and fund government-wide Blanket Purchase Agreements (BPA) used to provide Federal agencies a basic set of tools to support the continuous monitoring of information systems. Among these tools will be agency dashboards with customizable report functions and a Federal enterprise-wide dashboard that will allow DHS to improve its response to cyber threats. Once fully implemented, CDM will enable agencies to identify and respond, in near real-time, to cybersecurity challenges.

The rollout of CDM is organized into three phases designed to allow agencies to implement CDM in a consistent manner that demonstrates measureable cybersecurity results and leverages strategic sourcing to achieve cost savings. Phase One of CDM focuses on endpoint integrity and device management. Specifically, this phase encompasses the management of hardware and software assets, configuration management, and vulnerability management. These capabilities form an essential foundation on which the rest of CDM will build. As of the end of FY 2014, over 1.7 million licenses for these security monitoring tools and products had been purchased and distributed to agencies. This marked a major step in the implementation of CDM and demonstrated the efficiency of the BPA, which achieved $26 million in cost-avoidance when compared to the GSA General Schedule. Phase Two will focus on monitoring attributes of the authorized users operating in an agency's computing environment. This includes the individual's security clearance or suitability, security related training, and any privileged access they may possess. Phase Three will focus on boundary protection and response to cyber incidents and vulnerabilities. These capabilities will include audit and event detection/response, status of encryption, remote access, and access control of the environment.

National Cybersecurity Protection System (EINSTEIN)

The goal of the *National Cybersecurity Protection System* (EINSTEIN) is to provide the Federal Government with an early warning system, improved situational awareness of intrusion threats to Federal Executive Branch civilian networks, near real-time identification of malicious cyber activity, and prevention of that malicious cyber activity. Following widespread deployment of EINSTEIN 2, a passive intrusion detection system that issues alerts when threats are detected, DHS has begun deploying EINSTEIN 3 Accelerated (E3A), which will provide agencies an intrusion prevention capability with the ability to block and disable attempted intrusions before harm is done. By contracting with major Internet Service Providers (ISPs), the initial deployment of E3A is focused on countermeasures that will address approximately 85% of the cybersecurity threats affecting the Federal civilian networks. To date, the DHS Office of Cybersecurity and Communications has deployed E3A at seven departments and agencies. For FY 2015, DHS will continue this progress and build on experiences gained in FY 2014 to maintain positive momentum in providing advanced intrusion detection capabilities for government systems.

Additional Government-wide Programs Administered by Agencies

Facilitating Mobile Security

In FY 2014, NIST issued a series of guidelines to assist organizations in managing risks associated with the increased use of mobile devices, of which there are 4,171,168. In August 2014, NIST issued *Draft Special Publication (SP) 800-163, "Draft Technical Considerations for Vetting 3rd Party Mobile Applications"* to provide guidance for vetting 3rd party software applications (apps) for mobile devices. Mobile app vetting is intended to assess a mobile application's operational characteristics of secure behavior and reliability, including performance, so that organizations can determine if the app is acceptable for use in their expected environment. The draft SP provides key technical software assurance considerations for organizations as they adopt mobile app vetting processes.

NIST also issued *SP 800-101 Revision 1, "Guidelines on Mobile Device Forensics,"* to provide basic information on mobile forensics tools and the preservation, acquisition, examination, analysis, and reporting of digital evidence present on mobile devices. Additionally, NIST released Revision 1 of *SP 800-157, "Guidelines for Derived Personal Identity Verification (PIV) Credentials."* SP 800-157 defines a technical specification for implementing and deploying derived PIV credentials to mobile devices, such as smart phones and tablets. The goal of the derived PIV credential is to provide PIV-enabled authentication services from mobile devices to authenticate to remote systems. Along with SP 800-157, NIST published *Draft NIST Interagency Report (NISTIR) 7981, "Mobile, PIV, and Authentication,"* which provides an analysis and summary of various current and near-term options for remote authentication with mobile devices that leverage the investment in the PIV infrastructure and the unique security capabilities of mobile devices.

FedRAMP and the Safe, Secure Adoption of Cloud

To accelerate the adoption of cloud computing solutions across the Federal Government, on December 8, 2011, the Federal Chief Information Officer (CIO) published the *"Security Authorization of Information Systems in Cloud Computing Environments"* policy memorandum. This memorandum formally established the *Federal Risk and Authorization Management Program (FedRAMP),* a process that replaced the varied and duplicative cloud service assessment procedures across government by providing agencies with a standard approach. The approach is based on an accepted set of baseline security controls and consistent processes that have been vetted and agreed upon by agencies across the Federal Government. The memorandum established roles and responsibilities, implementation timelines, and requirements for agency compliance, including that all low and moderate impact cloud services leveraged by more than one office or agency comply with FedRAMP requirements.

In FY 2014, FedRAMP issued four Provisional Authorizations and six Agency Authorizations to Cloud Service Providers (CSP). A Provisional Authorization is an initial statement of risk and approval of an authorization package pending the issuance of a final authorization to operate by the agency acquiring the cloud service (Agency Authorization). Twenty-six agencies have reported using FedRAMP provisionally authorized packages, and agencies have reported a total of 81 systems as being FedRAMP compliant. In FY 2015, FedRAMP will pursue three main goals: (1) increase compliance and agency participation in FedRAMP; (2) improve the efficiency of the program by streamlining processes and other internal improvements; and (3) continue to adapt as the fast-moving landscape of securing cloud technology evolves.

National Strategy for Trusted Identities in Cyberspace (NSTIC) and Connect.gov

In response to demand for improved digital identification from the private sector, government, and the general public, the Administration released the *"National Strategy for Trusted Identities in Cyberspace"* (NSTIC) in April 2011. The NSTIC calls for public-private collaboration to create an Identity Ecosystem – a marketplace of more secure, convenient, interoperable, and privacy-enhancing solutions for online authentication and identification. The NSTIC outlines an approach for the Executive Branch to catalyze and facilitate the private sector's development of this online identity environment. This environment will allow individuals and organizations to utilize secure, efficient, easy-to-use, and interoperable identity solutions to access online services in a manner that promotes confidence, privacy, choice, and innovation.

In support of NSTIC, the United States Postal Service (USPS) and the General Services Administration (GSA) are administering *Connect.gov* (formerly known as the Federal Cloud Credential Exchange). *Connect.gov* is a secure, privacy-enhancing cloud service that conveniently connects individuals to online government services using an approved digital credential individuals may already possess and trust. Traditionally, individuals seeking to do business with the Federal Government had to create agency-specific user names and passwords to access information online.

Connect.gov allows an individual to access these same Government websites and services by signing in with a third-party credential whose identity services have been approved by GSA's Federal Identity, Credential, and Access Management (FICAM) Trust Framework Solutions program. This will eliminate the need for consumers to maintain multiple logins for government agencies, and will enable government to more effectively serve people through a wide array of new citizen-facing applications. In FY 2014, *Connect.gov* entered an operational pilot with the Department of Veterans Affairs (VA), the Department of Agriculture (USDA), and NIST to allow consumers to access internet applications using a digital credential issued by a government certified provider. Moving forward, *Connect.gov* will continue to integrate additional agencies and enter full operating capacity in FY 2015.

B. OMB'S ROLE IN FEDERAL CYBERSECURITY

Per FISMA, OMB E-Gov, under the direction of the Federal CIO, has possessed oversight responsibilities for Federal cybersecurity policy and implementation. As the need for greater coordination across government has grown to keep paces with increasing threats, OMB has increased its role in the process. This involvement has been multifaceted, ranging from overseeing the Federal response to cyber events like the Heartbleed and Bash vulnerabilities, to holding agency leadership accountable for cybersecurity performance through the PortfolioStat[1] and CyberStat initiatives.[2] Due to the rapidly evolving threat landscape and commitment by Congress to improve Federal cybersecurity, OMB recently created a dedicated unit within OMB E-Gov, the Cyber and National Security Unit (E-Gov Cyber), which will focus on strengthening Federal cybersecurity through targeted oversight and policy issuance.

E-Gov Cyber was made possible by Congress's continued commitment to improving Federal cybersecurity. Initially in FY 2014 and again in FY 2015, Congress provided OMB resources for improved cybersecurity oversight and analytics through the Information Technology Oversight and Reform (ITOR) fund.[3] E-Gov Cyber will focus on the following strategic objectives with its partners, the National Security Council (NSC) staff, DHS, and NIST:

- Data-driven, risk-based oversight of agency and government-wide cybersecurity programs;

- Issuance and implementation of Federal cybersecurity policies consistent with emerging technologies and evolving cyber threats;

- Oversight and coordination of the Federal response to major cyber incidents and vulnerabilities to ensure appropriate mitigation strategies are effectively implemented; and

- Engagement with key stakeholders to modernize relevant cybersecurity statutes.

In FY 2015, E-Gov Cyber will target oversight through CyberStat reviews based on agencies with high risk factors, as determined by cybersecurity performance and incident data. Through increased resources, OMB will be able to ensure that these reviews help equip agencies with the proper tools and processes to enhance their cybersecurity capabilities. The unit will remain focused on ensuring successful DHS implementation of critical programs such as the *National Cybersecurity Protection System (NCPS)* and *Continuous Diagnostics & Mitigation (CDM)*. Lastly, E-Gov Cyber will enhance OMB's ability to issue and update long standing Federal cybersecurity guidance, such as *Circular A-130*, to ensure agencies have the best practices and techniques at their disposal.

Persistent cyber threats remain a challenge for the Federal Government. Through the efforts described above, E-Gov Cyber will facilitate coordinated protection, response mechanisms, and close collaboration between Federal cybersecurity partners, the Government will be able to better mitigate the impact of attacks when they occur, so agencies can focus on successful mission execution.

SECTION II: STATE OF FEDERAL CYBERSECURITY

Section II of this report describes the current state of Federal cybersecurity. The section identifies FY 2014 agency-reported cybersecurity incident information, highlights specific initiatives the Federal Government is implementing to address these incidents, and provides a review of agency performance against these initiatives. Additionally, for the first time, E-Gov Cyber has provided specific analysis regarding agency performance against Strong Authentication goals. E-Gov Cyber's analysis indicates that nearly a third of Federal incidents are related to or could have been prevented by Strong Authentication implementation. This section concludes with an identification of next steps to address these challenges. Additional information on agency performance against cybersecurity initiatives and metrics can be found in **Appendix 3: FY 2014 CAP and FISMA Key Metrics Details**.

A. FY 2014 CYBERSECURITY INCIDENTS

US-CERT receives computer security incident reports from the Federal Government, state and local governments, commercial enterprises, U.S. citizens, and international Computer Security Incident Response Teams (CSIRTs).[4] A computer security incident within the Federal Government is defined by NIST and US-CERT as a violation or imminent threat of violation of computer security policies, acceptable use policies, or standard security practices. In accordance with Section 301 § 3544 of the E-Government Act of 2002, as well as additional requirements described in the *Updated DHS US-CERT Incident Notification Guidelines* subsection below, Federal agencies are required to notify US-CERT through the *US-CERT Incident Reporting System* upon the discovery of a computer security incident. The total number of computer security incidents for each group can be found in **Table 1** below.

Table 1: Incidents Reported to US-CERT in FY 2014

Reporting Source	Total Number of Incident Reports
Federal Government Total	69,851
Federal Government: CFO Act	67,196
Federal Government: Non-CFO Act	2,655
Non-Federal	570,371
TOTAL	**640,222**

Source: Data reported to US-CERT Incident Reporting System from October 1, 2013 to September 30, 2014.

Definitions for all types of computer security incidents are shown in **Table 2**. It should be noted that this table includes both computer security incident categories as well as selected subcategories. These distinguishable subcategories have been noted along with the larger category to which they belong.

Table 2: US-CERT FY 2014 Incident Definitions

Category/Subcategories	Definition
Denial of Service (DoS)	This category is used for all *successful* DoS attacks, such as a flood of traffic which renders a web server unavailable to legitimate users.
Improper Usage	Improper Usage categorizes all incidents where a user violates acceptable computing policies or rules of behavior. These include incidents like the spillage of information from one classification level to another.
-Unauthorized Access	Unauthorized Access is when individual gains logical or physical access without permission to a Federal agency network, system, application, data or other resource. (*Subcategory of Improper Usage Category*)
-Social Engineering	Social Engineering is used to categorize fraudulent web sites and other attempts to entice users to provide sensitive information or download malicious code. Phishing is a set of Social Engineering, which is itself a subcategory of Unauthorized Access. (*Set of Unauthorized Access Subcategory*)
-Phishing	Phishing is an attempt by an individual or group to solicit personal information from unsuspecting users by employing social engineering techniques, typically via emails containing links to fraudulent websites. (*Set of Social Engineering Subcategory*)
-Equipment	This set of Unauthorized Access is used for all incidents involving lost, stolen or confiscated equipment, including mobile devices, laptops, backup disks or removable media. (*Set of Unauthorized Access Subcategory*)
-Policy Violation	Policy Violation is primarily used to categorize incidents of mishandling data in storage or transit, such as digital PII records or procurement sensitive information found unsecured or PII being emailed without proper encryption. (*Subcategory of Improper Usage Category*)
Malicious Code	Used for all *successful* executions or installations of malicious software which are not immediately quarantined and cleaned by preventative measures such as antivirus tools.
Non Cyber	Non Cyber is used for filing all reports of PII spillages or possible mishandling of PII which involve hard copies or printed material as opposed to digital records.
Other	For the purposes of this report, a separate superset of multiple subcategories has been employed to accommodate several low-frequency types of incident reports, such as unconfirmed third-party notifications, failed brute force attempts, port scans, or reported incidents where the cause is unknown.
Suspicious Network Activity	This category is primarily utilized for incident reports and notifications created from EINSTEIN data analyzed by US-CERT.

Source: Classifications and definitions provided by US-CERT

CFO Act Agency Incidents Reported to US-CERT

During FY 2014, US-CERT processed 67,196 incidents reported by CFO Act agencies, up from 57,971 incidents reported by CFO Act agencies in FY 2013 as shown in **Figure 1** below. Although the rise in incidents warrants attention, it represents both an increase in total information security events as well as enhanced capabilities to identify, detect, manage, recover and respond to these incidents.

At 16,923 incidents (25% of reported incidents) in FY 2014, Non-Cyber, a category which includes the mishandling of sensitive information without a cybersecurity component, such as the loss of hard copy Personal Identity Information (PII) records, was the most frequently reported incident type by CFO Act agencies. The second most reported category was Other, which includes incidents such as scans, probes and attempted access, incidents under investigation, and incidents categorized as miscellaneous categories such as General Public or Joint Indicator Bulletin (JIB). The Other category represented 14,530, or 22% of reported incidents. The third most reported category was Policy Violations, which represented 11,614 reported incidents, or 17% of total incidents reported. CFO Act agency-specific data can be found in **Appendix 2** of this report.

Figure 1: Summary of CFO Act Agency Incidents Reported to US-CERT in FY 2013 & FY 2014

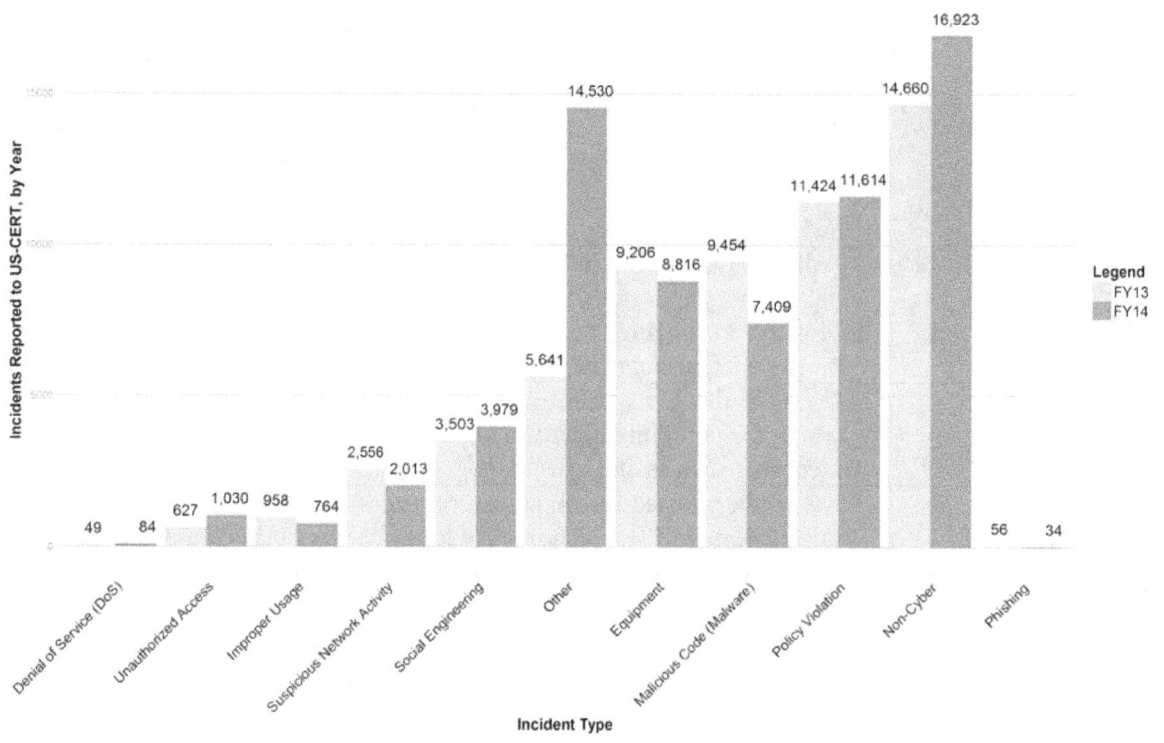

Source: Data reported to US-CERT Incident Reporting System from October 1, 2012, to September 30, 2014.

Non-CFO Act Agency Incidents Reported to US-CERT

During FY 2014, US-CERT processed 2,655 incidents reported by non-CFO Act agencies, the specifics of which are shown in **Figure 2** below. At 561 incidents (21% of reported incidents), Suspicious Network Activity, which is primarily comprised of incident reports and notifications created from EINSTEIN data, was the largest category of incidents reported by Non-CFO Act agencies in FY 2014. Equipment, all incidents involving lost, stolen or confiscated equipment, including mobile devices, laptops, backup disks or removable media, was the next most frequently reported incident in FY 2014 with 492 reported incidents, or 19% of total incidents. The third most frequently reported incident type was Policy Violations, which includes the mishandling of data storage and transmission, with 488 reported incidents, or 18% of total incidents.

Figure 2: Summary of Non-CFO Act Agency Incidents Reported to US-CERT in FY 2013 & FY 2014

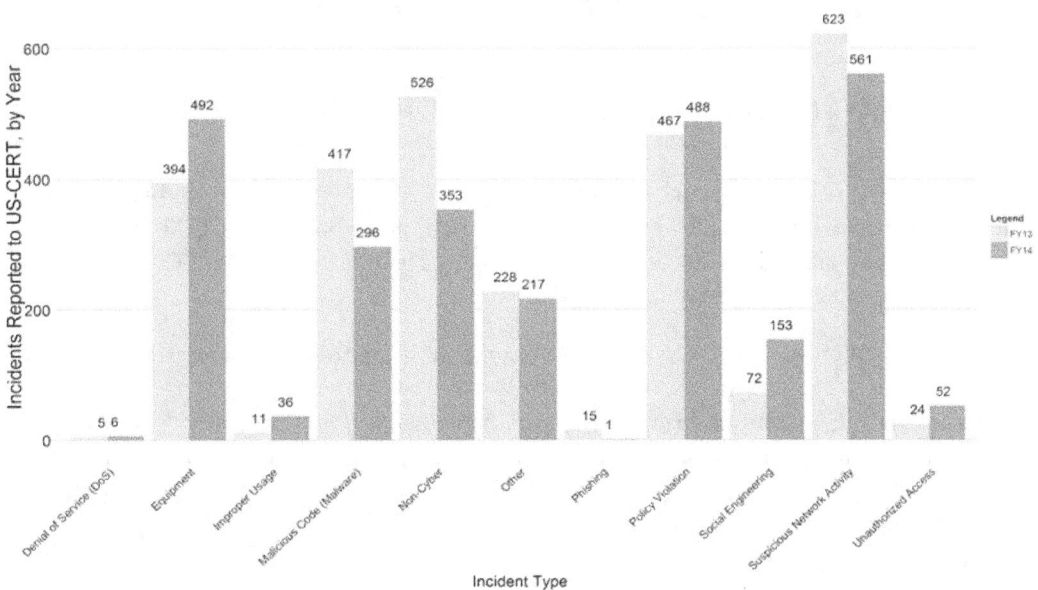

Source: Data reported to US-CERT Incident Reporting System from October 1, 2012, to September 30, 2014.

Updated DHS US-CERT Incident Notification Guidelines

Throughout FY 2013 and FY 2014, US-CERT worked with OMB, NSC staff, Federal agencies, and the Federal CIO Council's Information Security Identity Management Committee (ISIMC) to streamline the incident reporting process to improve the quality of incident data. OMB Memorandum M-15-01, *"Fiscal Year 2014-2015 Guidance on Improving Federal Information Security and Privacy Management Practices,"* formally issued US-CERT's updated Incident Notification Guidelines, which went into effect at the beginning of FY 2015. The updated guidelines will be non-binding for agencies throughout FY 2015 while agencies transition away from the legacy reporting methodology. Because these changes were not announced until the beginning of FY 2015, this report identifies incidents using the *legacy incident reporting category system* referenced above. As this transition continues, future OMB FISMA reports will identify Federal incidents using the new guidelines, where possible.

These guidelines support US-CERT in executing its mission objectives and enable the following benefits:

- Greater quality of information - Alignment with incident reporting and handling guidance from *NIST SP 800-61, Revision 2, "Computer Security Incident Handling Guide,"* to introduce functional, informational and recoverability impact classifications, allowing US-CERT to better recognize significant incidents.

- Improved information sharing and situational awareness - Establishing a one-hour notification time frame for all incidents to improve US-CERT's ability to understand cybersecurity events affecting the government.

- Faster incident response times - Moving cause analysis to the closing phase of the incident handling process to expedite initial notification.

To ensure the guidelines remain up to date in addressing dynamic cybersecurity challenges, DHS US-CERT committed to establishing a schedule for reviewing and updating the incident notification guidelines at regular intervals in coordination with OMB and the Federal CIO Council.

B. AGENCY CYBERSECURITY CAP GOAL PERFORMANCE

Recognizing the continued risk cybersecurity incidents pose to Federal information and information systems, OMB, in coordination with NSC staff and DHS, developed the Cybersecurity CAP goal for FY 2012 to FY 2014, which can be viewed on *www.Performance.gov*. The Cybersecurity CAP represents the basic building blocks of a strong cybersecurity program.

The FY 2012 to FY 2014 Cybersecurity CAP goal is comprised of the following initiatives:

- **Information Security Continuous Monitoring (ISCM) –** *Know Your Network*

  ISCM is designed to combat information security threats by maintaining ongoing awareness of information security, vulnerabilities, and threats to Federal systems and information. ISCM demands ongoing observation, assessment, analysis, and diagnosis of an organization's cybersecurity posture and operational readiness.

- **Strong Authentication –** *Know Your Users*

  The goal of Strong Authentication is to use identification authentication technology to ensure that access to Federal systems and resources is limited to users who require it as part of their job function. Strong Authentication requires multiple factors to securely authenticate a user: (1) something the user has, such as a PIV card; (2) something the user is, an approved user; and (3) something the user knows, such as a password or key code.

- **Trusted Internet Connection (TIC) Consolidation and TIC 2.0 Capabilities –** *Know Your Traffic*

  The goal of TIC is to protect the data and information entering and exiting Federal networks, and to identify network connections that may pose a security risk. TIC Consolidation requires that agencies consolidate the number of internet access points into a limited number of trusted connections. *TIC 2.0* Capabilities tracks the percentage of implemented TIC 2.0 capabilities; a body of 60 critical capabilities that were collaboratively developed to improve upon baseline security requirements.

CFO Act performance against the Cybersecurity CAP goal is described in the following tables by ranking agencies from the lowest to the highest performing.

As seen in **Table 3** below, significant progress was made in FY 2014 toward meeting the ISCM CAP goal target of 95% implementation, with average CFO Act agency performance improving from 81% in FY 2013 to 92% in FY 2014. While the improvement in performance is encouraging, average performance still failed to meet the established goal of 95%. The blue cells indicate agencies that did not meet this target. For a list of CFO Act agency abbreviations, see **Appendix 6: List of CFO Act Agencies**.

Table 3: ISCM Capabilities FY 2013 & FY 2014

Agency	Information Security Continuous Monitoring Average FY 2013 (%)	Information Security Continuous Monitoring Average FY 2014 (%)
HHS	90	80
EPA	57	82
DOT	52	88
Commerce	69	88
NRC	95	89
DOD	76	90
USAID	97	90
HUD	85	91
Energy	86	92
Interior	86	94
DHS	94	95
State	82	95
VA	77	96
NSF	95	96
NASA	88	96
OPM	97	97
SSA	96	98
Treasury	84	98
ED	95	98
GSA	98	98
Labor	97	99
Justice	99	99
USDA	100	100
SBA	63	100
CFO Act Agency Average*	81	92

*The average is weighted by the total number of the agency's hardware assets connected to the agency's unclassified network(s).
Source: Analysis of FISMA Agency Level Questions Data (Questions 2.1, 2.2, and 4.1), and FISMA Agency Level Secure Configuration Management Assets and Percentage Data (Questions 3.1.2 and 3.1.3), reported to DHS via CyberScope from October 1, 2012, to September 30, 2014.

As seen in **Table 4** below, numerous agencies have made no progress meeting the Strong Authentication CAP goal. SBA, NRC, HUD, Labor, and State were all at 0% Strong Authentication implementation at the end of FY 2014. The blue cells indicate performance that fell below the 75% target across all CFO Act agencies. Excluding DOD, the percentage of CFO Act agency users for whom Strong Authentication is required is 41%.[5]

Table 4: Strong Authentication Capabilities FY 2013 & FY 2014

Agency	Strong Authentication FY 2013 (%)	Strong Authentication FY 2014 (%)
Labor	0	0
HUD	0	0
NRC	0	0
SBA	0	0
State	1	0
OPM	0	1
USAID	0	3
USDA	6	6
VA	4	10
NSF	0	19
Energy	9	29
DOT	7	31
Interior	0	36
Treasury	9	43
Justice	30	44
EPA	0	69
HHS	66	69
DHS	30	80
NASA	17	82
ED	75	85
SSA	85	85
DOD	89	87
Commerce	30	88
GSA	94	95
CFO Act Agency Average*	67	72

*The average is weighted by the total number of people at the agency who have network accounts.
Source: Analysis of FISMA Agency Level Questions Data (Questions 5.1, 5.2.5, 5.3, and 5.4.5), reported to DHS via CyberScope from October 1, 2012, to September 30, 2014.

As seen in **Table 5** below, the TIC Consolidation initiative CAP goal was met by most agencies in FY 2014, with the CFO Act agency average standing at the 95% goal of external network traffic passing through a TIC or Managed Trusted Internet Protocol Services (MTIPS) provider. Twenty agencies met or exceeded the CAP goal in FY 2014 with only three agencies, VA (57%), Energy (72%), and Commerce (86%), failing to meet the established target, indicated in blue cells below. Note that DOD implemented a similar initiative on its networks, and is therefore exempted from measurement on TIC Traffic Consolidation and TIC 2.0 Capabilities.

Table 5: TIC Traffic Consolidation FY 2013 & FY 2014

Agency	TIC Traffic Consolidation FY 2013 (%)	TIC Traffic Consolidation FY 2014 (%)
DOD*	N/A	N/A
VA	39	57
Energy	26	72
Commerce	76	86
ED	91	95
EPA	95	95
DHS	94	97
HHS	0	98
DOT	99	99
Treasury	99	99
NASA	100	99
SBA	100	99
USDA	71	100
Interior	99	100
Justice	99	100
Labor	100	100
GSA	100	100
HUD	100	100
OPM	100	100
SSA	100	100
State	100	100
USAID	100	100
NRC	100	100
NSF	100	100
CFO Act Agency Average	86	95

*DOD implemented an initiative similar to TIC and is therefore exempted from measurement on TIC Traffic Consolidation and TIC 2.0 Capabilities.

Source: Analysis of FISMA Agency Level Questions Data (Question 7.2), reported to DHS via CyberScope from October 1, 2012, to September 30, 2014.

As seen in **Table 6** below, CFO Act Agency performance fell short of the 100% target for FY 2014, although significant improvement was made from 87% implementation in FY 2013 to 92% in FY 2014. The following agencies met 100% of the target: Labor, NRC, NSF, and SBA. However, most agencies failed to reach the target, with HHS (74%), Commerce (75%), and OPM (77%) reporting the lowest percentage among the CFO Act agencies. The blue cells indicate performance that fell below the 100% target.

Table 6: TIC 2.0 Capabilities FY 2013 & FY 2014

Agency	TIC 2.0 Capabilities FY 2013 (%)	TIC 2.0 Capabilities FY 2014 (%)
DOD*	N/A	N/A
HHS	100	74
Commerce	41	75
OPM	82	77
DOT	72	85
Justice	93	88
USDA	82	89
NASA	88	89
EPA	90	90
Interior	86	91
DHS	92	92
USAID	92	92
State	78	93
VA	82	93
SSA	96	94
ED	85	95
Energy	92	96
HUD	68	98
GSA	100	98
Treasury	93	99
Labor	100	100
NRC	100	100
NSF	100	100
SBA	100	100
CFO Act Agency Average	87	92

*DOD implemented an initiative similar to TIC and is therefore exempted from measurement on TIC Traffic Consolidation and TIC 2.0 Capabilities.

Source: Analysis of FISMA Agency Level Questions Data (Question 7.1), reported to DHS via CyberScope from October 1, 2012, to September 30, 2014.

Overall, Cybersecurity CAP goal performance has improved greatly since OMB began measuring performance in FY 2012. However, agency implementation of Strong Authentication remains a key concern. As highlighted in **Table 4** above, 15 agencies have yet to reach even 50% implementation on the Strong Authentication initiative. When removing DOD from the government-wide average, only 41% of agency user accounts require Strong Authentication. This statistic is significant due to the fact that major cyber incidents can often be tied to the lack of Strong Authentication implementation, as detailed below.

C. E-GOV CYBER STRONG AUTHENTICATION ANALYSIS

In the wake of increasing cyber threats and high-profile data breaches, E-Gov Cyber conducted an analysis of agency incident and performance data to determine where to focus its oversight efforts in FY 2015. E-Gov Cyber found during its analysis that the majority of Federal cybersecurity incidents are related to or could potentially have been mitigated by Strong Authentication implementation. Using the US-CERT incident definitions described at the beginning of this section, E-Gov Cyber grouped incidents into four categories to more easily determine whether or not they were related to or could have been allayed by the implementation of Strong Authentication. The incident types are as follows:

- Improper Usage, Suspicious Network Activity, and Unauthorized Access – Improper user behavior can be deterred by reducing anonymity through Strong Authentication.

- Social Engineering, Phishing, and Malicious Code – These incident types can be deterred through use of PIV card capabilities like digitally signing emails, and delivering corresponding user training to thwart phishing attempts.

- Denial of Service, Equipment, and Other – These incident types are not typically related to Strong Authentication implementation.

- Non-Cyber – This incident type was removed from E-Gov Cyber's analysis since it is not related to cybersecurity incidents.

Based on the above incident groupings, US-CERT incident reports indicate that in FY 2013, 65% of Federal civilian cybersecurity incidents were related to or could have been prevented by Strong Authentication implementation. This figure decreased 13% in FY 2014 to 52% of cyber incidents reported to US-CERT.[6] While this is a decrease from FY 2013, it is still a troublingly high percentage when one considers that Strong Authentication implementation for civilian agency user accounts remains at only 41%, well below the 75% target.

Network Access: Password vs. PIV Card

Using the incident statistics as the starting point for its analysis, E-Gov Cyber reviewed agency performance against authentication-related Key FISMA Metrics (KFMs). As part of the FISMA reporting process, agencies report the different methods by which users are able to gain access to Federal information and networks. **Figure 3** below identifies the number of users at each CFO Act agency who are able to log on with just a user ID and password versus the number that are required to log on with a two-factor PIV Card (excluding DOD[7]).

Agencies which have the weakest authentication profile allow the majority of unprivileged users to log on with user ID and password alone, which makes unauthorized network access more likely as passwords are much easier to steal through either malicious software or social engineering. The following 16 agencies fall into this category: State, Labor, HUD, OPM, NRC, SBA, NSF, USAID, USDA, Energy, DOT, Interior, VA, Justice, Treasury, and NASA.

Figure 3: Unprivileged Network Accounts: Password vs. PIV Card

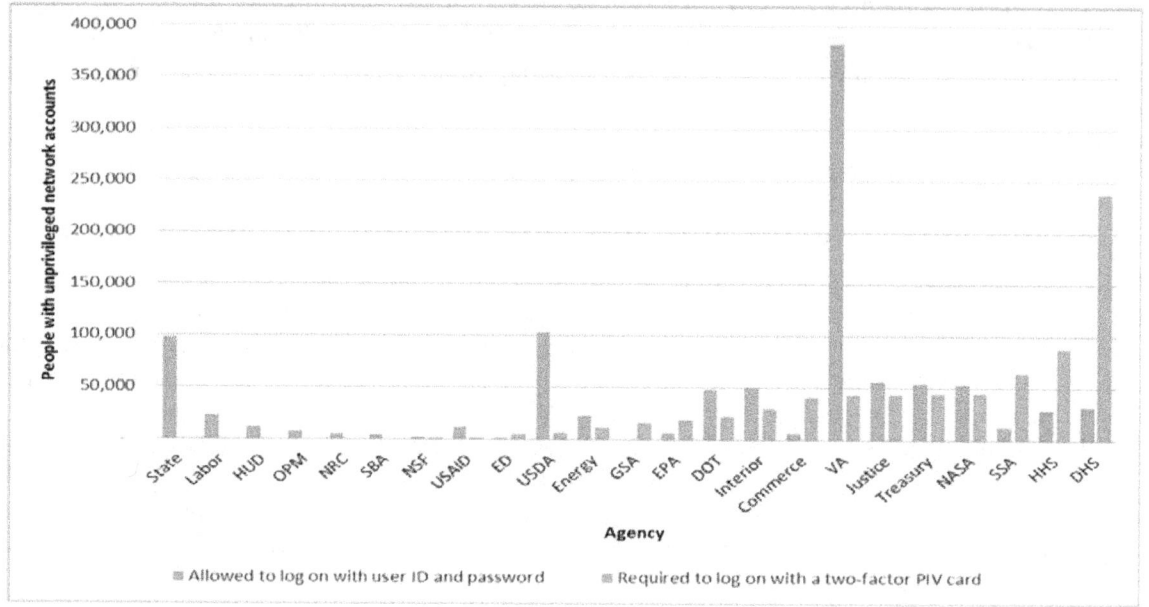

Source: Analysis of FISMA Agency Level Questions Data (Questions 5.1, 5.2.1, and 5.2.5) reported to DHS via CyberScope from October 1, 2013 to September 30, 2014

While the substantial number of unprivileged user accounts, of which there are 5,325,374 government-wide, that are able to log on to Federal networks with only a user ID and password is concerning, a potentially more serious issue is the number of privileged network accounts that are able to log on with only a user ID and password. Privileged user accounts, of which there are 134,287 across the Federal Government, possess elevated levels of access to or control of Federal systems and information, significantly increasing the risk to Government resources if their credentials are compromised. **Figure 4** below identifies this data (excluding DOD[8]). The following 18 agencies do not require a majority of their privileged network users to log on using two-factor PIV authentication: State, VA, USDA, EPA, Labor, HUD, GSA, USAID, SBA, NRC, NASA, DOT, Treasury, HHS, Energy, Justice, Interior, and DHS.

Figure 4: Privileged Network Accounts: Password vs. PIV Card

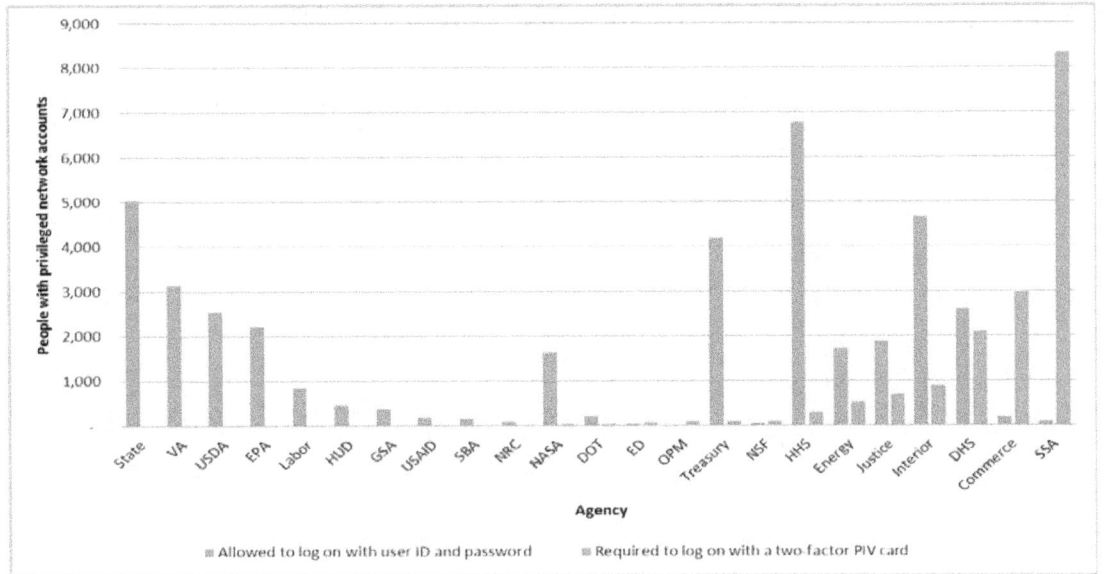

Source: Analysis of FISMA Agency Level Questions Data (Questions 5.3, 5.4.1, and 5.4.5) reported to DHS via CyberScope from October 1, 2013, to September 30, 2014

While the CAP goal metrics and additional metrics on strong authentication described above are particularly important in protecting Federal information and systems, there are additional Key FISMA Metrics (KFMs) which contribute to a more comprehensive understanding of agency performance. Appendix 3 identifies both agency CAP goal as well as KFMs performance. More specific information on each of these metrics is also available online at the *DHS FY 2014 CIO Annual FISMA Metrics page*. Agency performance on these metrics, combined with relevant incident data from US-CERT, will inform how E-Gov Cyber prioritizes its oversight activities in FY 2015. For instance, E-Gov Cyber is prioritizing the agencies which have encountered difficulty in implementing Strong Authentication for CyberStat reviews to ensure agencies are adequately addressing this basic building block of cybersecurity.

SECTION III: SUMMARY OF INSPECTORS GENERAL'S FINDINGS

Each agency's Inspector General (IG) was asked to assess his or her department's information security programs in 11 areas and upload their information into CyberScope. These 11 areas were:

- Continuous monitoring management;

- Configuration management;

- Identity and access management;

- Incident response and reporting;

- Risk management;

- Security training;

- Plans of action and milestones (POA&M);

- Remote access management;

- Contingency planning;

- Contractor systems; and

- Security capital planning

The assessment consisted of two parts: (1) determining if a program was in place for the area, and (2) evaluating 104 attributes.[9] It is important to note that the Inspectors General assessment is separate from the assessment conducted by OMB, which is done in coordination with DHS. The two assessments are based on differing methodologies, where the IGs assess the existence of information security program components, and OMB and DHS assess, through the FISMA metrics, program quality and degree of implementation. The following summarizes IG results for (1) CFO Act agencies and (2) small and micro agencies. Appendix 4, Inspectors General's Summary, provides additional details.

CFO Act Agencies

As shown in **Table 7**, the majority of CFO Act agencies have programs in each of the 11 cybersecurity areas. Twenty or more agencies have programs in place for incident response and reporting, remote access, and/or security training. Programs not in place were more prevalent in the areas of configuration management, identity and access management, and risk management, with up to eight agencies not having one or more of these programs.

Table 7: Status of Agency Programs by Cybersecurity Area

	Cyber Security Program Area	Program in place		Program not in place	
		No.	%	No.	%
1	Continuous monitoring	19	79%	5	21%
2	Configuration management	16	67%	8	33%
3	Identity and access management	16	67%	8	33%
4	Incident response and reporting	21	88%	3	13%
5	Risk management	17	71%	7	29%
6	Security training	20	83%	4	17%
7	POA&M	19	79%	5	21%
8	Remote access management	21	88%	3	13%
9	Contingency planning *	17	74%	6	26%
10	Contractor systems *	17	74%	6	26%
11	Security capital planning *	19	83%	4	17%

Source: Data provided to DHS via CyberScope from November 15, 2012, to November 14, 2014.
* One OIG did not report on these programs; therefore, only 23 agencies are included in these areas.

Table 8 provides the CFO Act agencies' cybersecurity assessment scores for fiscal years 2014, 2013 and 2012. The scores are based on (1) whether or not a program was in place for each area, and (2) how many attributes were found in each agency's cybersecurity program. The table is ordered by FY 2014 scores. Eight agencies scored over 90% (green), which is an increase of three from FY 2013, but the same as FY 2012. Eight agencies scored between 65% and 90% (yellow), and the remaining six scored lower than 65% (red). Commerce[10] and DOD[11] were not scored. The average score for reporting agencies was 76% for FY 2014—the same as in FY 2013.

Table 8: CFO Act Agencies' Scores

Agency	FY 2014 (%)	FY 2013 (%)	FY 2012 (%)
General Services Administration	99	98	99
Department of Justice	99	98	94
Department of Homeland Security	98	99	99
Nuclear Regulatory Commission	96	98	99
Social Security Administration	96	96	98
National Aeronautics and Space Administration	95	91	92
Department of the Interior	92	79	92
Department of Education	91	89	79
National Science Foundation	87	88	90
United States Agency for International Development (USAID)	86	83	66
Environmental Protection Agency	84	77	77
Department of Labor	82	76	82
Department of Veteran Affair	80	81	81
Department of Energy	78	75	72
Office of Personnel Management	74	83	77
Department of the Treasury	67	76	76
Department of Transportation	63	61	53
Small Business Administration	58	55	57
U.S. Department of Agriculture	53	37	34
Department of State	42	51	53
Department of Health and Human Services	35	43	50
Department of Housing and Urban Development	19	29	66
Department of Defense	N/A*	N/A*	N/A*
Department of Commerce	N/A†	87	61

Source: Data provided to DHS via CyberScope from November 15, 2012, to November 14, 2014.
* Due to the size of the Department, the DOD OIG is unable to definitively report a yes or no answer for all FISMA attributes.
† Commerce OIG's FISMA audit scope was reduced as a result of (1) attrition of several key IT security staff, (2) the need to complete audit work assessing the security posture of key weather satellite systems that support a national critical mission, and (3) additional office priorities. As a result, the FISMA submission primarily focused on assessing policies and procedures, and covered a limited number of systems that would not warrant computation of a compliance score.

Small and Micro Agencies

The results for the small and micro agencies were comparable to those of the 24 CFO Act agencies. **Table 9** summarizes the results from the IGs of the small and micro agencies according to cyber security program area. These results indicate that the small and micro agencies performed best (i.e., had programs in place) in security training, incident response and reporting, identity and access management, and remote access management. The weakest performances (i.e., highest number of cases where programs were not in place) occurred in risk management, continuous monitoring management, contingency planning and configuration management.

Table 9: Results for Small and Micro Agencies by Cyber Security Area

Cyber Security Program Area	Program in place		Program not in place	
	FY 2014	%	FY 2014	%
Continuous monitoring	22	58	16	42
Configuration management	25	66	13	34
Identity and access management	29	76	9	24
Incident response and reporting	30	79	8	21
Risk management	22	58	16	42
Security training	31	82	7	18
POA&M	27	71	11	29
Remote access management	29	76	9	24
Contingency planning	24	63	14	37
Contractor systems	26	68	12	32
Security capital planning	28	74	10	26

Source: Data provided to DHS via CyberScope from November 15, 2012, to November 14, 2014.

Table 10 provides the small and micro agencies' compliance scores for FY 2014 and FY 2013. The table is organized according to agencies' FY 2014 compliance scores. These agencies were scored using the same method applied to the CFO Act agencies. Twelve agencies scored over 90% (green), 12 scored between 65 and 90% compliance (yellow), and the remaining 14 scored less than 65% (red). Four small and micro agencies did not provide data. The average score was 73% for fiscal year 2014, which is comparable to the CFO Act agencies.

Table 10: Micro Agencies' Compliance Scores

Agency	FY 2014 (%)	FY 2013 (%)
Federal Energy Regulatory Commission	100	99
National Transportation Safety Board	100	78
Selective Service System	100	N/A
Overseas Private Investment Corporation	98	84
National Endowment for the Arts	98	N/A
Export-Import Bank of the United States	98	96
Equal Employment Opportunity Commission	95	99
National Credit Union Administration	95	83
Commodity Futures Trading Commission	95	81
Federal Housing Finance Agency	95	95
Millennium Challenge Corporation	94	84
Farm Credit Administration	92	99
Federal Trade Commission	91	92
National Endowment for the Humanities	90	87
Smithsonian Institution	87	88
Federal Reserve Board	87	88
Merit Systems Protection Board	83	88
Tennessee Valley Authority	82	99
Federal Deposit Insurance Corporation	82	87
Consumer Financial Protection Bureau	81	72
Securities and Exchange Commission	77	80
Railroad Retirement Board	73	80
International Boundary and Water Commission	72	53
Federal Labor Relations Authority	70	84
Federal Maritime Commission	66	54
Federal Mediation and Conciliation Service	65	65
Pension Benefit Guaranty Corporation	64	71
National Labor Relations Board	59	87
International Trade Commission	57	51
Corporation for National and Community Service	57	72
Armed Forces Retirement Home	56	N/A
Peace Corps	48	33
Defense Nuclear Facilities Safety Board	47	N/A
Broadcasting Board of Governors	47	50
Court Services and Offender Supervision Agency	39	71
Consumer Product Safety Commission	36	30
Federal Communications Commission	36	N/A
National Archives and Records Administration	16	N/A
Federal Retirement Thrift Investment Board	N/A	N/A
Federal Election Commission	N/A	N/A
Office of Special Counsel	N/A	N/A
Other Defense Civil Programs	N/A	74

Source: Data provided to DHS via CyberScope from November 15, 2012, to November 14, 2014.

NOTE: Federal Retirement Thrift Investment Board, Federal Election Commission, and Office of Special Counsel did not provide the answers with the detail required for scoring for FY 2014. Other Defense Civil Programs did not report answers for FY 2014.

SECTION IV: PROGRESS IN MEETING KEY PRIVACY PERFORMANCE MEASURES

Protecting individual privacy remains a top Administration priority. With the Federal Government's increasing use of information technology to collect, maintain, and disseminate personal information, Federal agencies must take steps to analyze and address privacy risks at the earliest stages of the planning process, and they must continue to manage information responsibly throughout the life cycle of the information.

Federal agencies must continue to work closely with their Senior Agency Official for Privacy (SAOP) to ensure compliance with all privacy requirements in law, regulation, and policy. Agencies are responsible for ensuring that all of their privacy impact assessments (PIAs) and system of records notices (SORNs) are completed and up to date. Moreover, agencies must continue to develop and implement policies that outline rules of behavior, detail training requirements for personnel, and identify consequences and corrective actions to address non-compliance. Finally, agencies must continue to implement appropriate data breach response procedures and update those procedures as needed.

Across the Federal Government, agencies are expected to demonstrate continued progress in all aspects of privacy protection. In order to more fully examine agencies' compliance with privacy requirements, this section of the report has been expanded to include results for not only CFO Act agencies, but also non-CFO Act agencies that reported privacy performance measures to OMB. In FY 2014, 24 CFO Act agencies and 41 non-CFO Act agencies reported privacy performance measures to OMB.

As can be seen in **Table 11** and **Table 12** below, the FY 2014 agency FISMA reports indicate that the Federal Government has made improvements in many privacy performance measures.

Table 11: CFO Act Agencies' Progress in Meeting Key Privacy Performance Measures

Key Privacy Performance Measures – CFO Act Agencies	FY 2012	FY 2013	FY 2014
Number of systems containing information in identifiable form	4,941	4,395	4,406
Number of systems requiring a Privacy Impact Assessment (PIA)	2,778	2,586	2,701
Number of systems with a PIA	2,612	2,436	2,564
Percentage of systems with a PIA	**94%**	**94%**	**95%**
Number of systems requiring a System of Records Notice (SORN)	3,498	3,343	3,346
Number of systems with a SORN	3,339	3,196	3,217
Percentage of systems with a SORN	**95%**	**96%**	**96%**

Source: Data reported to DHS via CyberScope and provided to the Office of Information and Regulatory Affairs (OIRA) from October 1, 2013, to September 30, 2014.

Table 12: Non-CFO Act Agencies' Progress in Meeting Key Privacy Performance Measures

Key Privacy Performance Measures – Non-CFO Act Agencies	FY 2014
Number of systems containing information in identifiable form	758
Number of systems requiring a Privacy Impact Assessment (PIA)	529
Number of systems with a PIA	436
Percentage of systems with a PIA	**82%**
Number of systems requiring a System of Records Notice (SORN)	605
Number of systems with a SORN	553
Percentage of systems with a SORN	**91%**

Source: Data reported to DHS via CyberScope and provided to the Office of Information and Regulatory Affairs (OIRA) from October 1, 2013, to September 30, 2014.

Privacy Program Oversight by the Senior Agency Official for Privacy

In FY 2014, 22 of 24 CFO Act agencies' SAOPs reported participation in all three privacy responsibility categories: privacy compliance activities; assessments of information technology; and evaluating legislative, regulatory, and other agency policy proposals for privacy. One CFO Act agency reported SAOP participation in two out of three categories and one agency reported no participation by the SAOP in any of the categories. Of the non-CFO Act agencies that reported privacy measures to OMB, 28 SAOPs reported participation in all three privacy responsibility categories, while five reported participation in two categories, two reported participation in one category, and six reported no participation in any of the three categories.

In addition, **Table 13** below shows the percentage of CFO Act and non-CFO Act agency SAOPs that provided formal written advice or guidance in each of the following categories:

Table 13: SAOP Formal Written Advice and Guidance

SAOP Provided Formal Written Advice or Guidance on:	CFO Act Agencies	Non-CFO Act Agencies
Agency policies, orders, directives, or guidance governing the agency's handling of PII	96%	90%
Written agreements (either interagency or with non-Federal entities) pertaining to information sharing, computer matching, and similar issues	83%	63%
Agency's practices for conducting, preparing, and releasing SORNs and PIAs	96%	73%
Reviews or feedback outside of the SORN and PIA process (e.g., formal written advice in the context of budgetary or programmatic activities or planning)	88%	66%
Privacy training (either stand-alone or combined with training on related issues)	42%	37%

Source: Data reported to DHS via CyberScope and provided to OIRA from October 1, 2013, to September 30, 2014.

Mandated Policy Compliance Reviews

The Privacy Act of 1974 (5 U.S.C. § 522a.), the E-Government Act of 2002 (44 U.S.C. §101 et seq.), and OMB guidance require Federal agencies to conduct certain reviews. In FY 2014, 23 out of 24 CFO Act agencies reported having current documentation demonstrating review of the agency's compliance with information privacy laws, regulations, and policies. Similarly, 23 out of 24 CFO Act agencies reported having documentation demonstrating review of planned, in progress, or completed corrective actions necessary to remedy deficiencies identified during compliance reviews. All but four CFO Act agencies reported using technologies that enable continuous auditing of compliance with their stated privacy policies and practices and all but one reported coordinating with their respective agency's Inspector General on privacy program oversight.

Thirty-two of the 41 non-CFO Act agencies that reported FY 2014 privacy performance measures to OMB reported coordinating with their respective agency's Inspector General on privacy program oversight, having current documentation demonstrating review of the agency's compliance with information privacy laws, regulations, and policies, as well as planned, in progress, or completed corrective actions necessary to remedy deficiencies identified during compliance reviews. Only 19 non-CFO Act agencies reported using technologies that enable continuous auditing of compliance with their stated privacy policies and practices.

Privacy Impact Assessments

The Federal Government's goal is for 100% of applicable systems to be covered by PIAs. In FY 2014, 95% of applicable systems reported by CFO Act agencies and 82% of applicable systems reported by non-CFO Act agencies had up-to-date PIAs. The 95% figure reported by CFO Act agencies marks the third consecutive year that compliance has improved across those agencies. In addition, all CFO Act agencies reported having a centrally located page on the agency's web site that provides working links to agency PIAs. Of the non-CFO Act agencies that reported having systems that require a PIA, six reported not having a centrally located page that provides working links to the agency PIAs.

Table 14 below shows the percentage of agencies that have reported having written policies or processes in place for the following privacy practices in FY 2014:

Table 14: Formal Agency Policies and Practices for PIAs

Have Written Policies or Processes in Place for:	CFO Act Agencies	Non-CFO Act Agencies
Determining whether a PIA is needed	100%	88%
Conducting a PIA	100%	85%
Evaluating changes in technology or business practices that are identified during the PIA process	100%	78%
Ensuring systems owners, privacy officials, and IT experts participate in conducting the PIA	100%	85%
Making PIAs available to the public as required by law and OMB policy	100%	73%
Monitoring the agency's systems and practices to determine when and how PIAs should be updated	100%	76%
Assessing the quality and thoroughness of each PIA and performing reviews to ensure that appropriate standards for PIAs are maintained	100%	80%

Source: Data reported to DHS via CyberScope and provided to the OIRA from October 1, 2013, to September 30, 2014.

System of Records Notices

The goal for the Federal Government is to cover 100% of applicable systems in which agencies maintain records subject to the Privacy Act with a published and up-to-date SORN. In FY 2014, 96% of CFO Act agencies' and 91% of non-CFO Act agencies' systems with Privacy Act records have a published, up-to-date SORN. In addition, all CFO Act agencies reported having a centrally located page on the agency's web site that provides working links to agency SORNs. Of the non-CFO Act agencies that reported having systems that require a SORN, four reported not having a centrally located page that provides working links to published SORNs.

Privacy Training

All 24 CFO Act agencies reported having a program to ensure that all personnel who handle personal information, who are directly involved in the administration of personal information or information technology systems, or that have significant information security responsibilities, receive job-specific and comprehensive information privacy training. Twenty-three of 24 CFO Act agencies reported having a policy in place to ensure that all personnel with access to Federal data are generally familiar with information privacy laws, regulations, and policies, and understand the ramifications of inappropriate access and disclosure. Thirty-eight non-CFO Act agencies also reported having such a policy.

Web Site Privacy Policies and Use of Web Management and Customization Technologies

In FY 2014, 23 out of 24 CFO Act agencies reported the use of web management and customization technologies. All 23 of those agencies reported having procedures for annual review, continued justification and approval, and public notice of their use of web management and customization technologies. In addition, 24 of the non-CFO Act agencies that reported privacy performance measures to OMB reported use of web management and customization technologies. Of those 24 agencies, 19 agencies reported having procedures for annual review, 23 agencies reported procedures for continued justification and approval, and all 24 reported having provided public notice of their use of such technologies.

Table 15 demonstrates the categories for which agencies reported having written policies or processes in place in FY 2014:

Table 15: Formal Agency Web Policies and Practices

Have Written Policies or Processes in Place for:	CFO Act Agencies	Non-CFO Act Agencies
Making appropriate updates and ensuring continued compliance with stated web privacy policies	100%	78%
Determining circumstances where the agency's web-based activities warrant additional consideration of privacy implications	100%	76%
Requiring machine-readability of public-facing organization web sites (i.e., use of P3P)	88%	76%

Source: Data reported to DHS via CyberScope and provided to the OIRA from October 1, 2013, to September 30, 2014.

SECTION V: APPENDICES

APPENDIX 1: NIST PERFORMANCE IN FY 2014

Section 301, §3543 of the E-Government Act of 2002 requires "an assessment of the development, promulgation, adoption of, and compliance with standards developed under Section 20 of the National Institute of Standards and Technology Act." Since the passage of the E- Government Act of 2002, NIST has worked to comply with FISMA requirements detailed in Section 303 of the Act. This includes developing and updating standards and guidelines for information systems used or operated by Federal agencies, providing agencies with technical assistance as requested, conducting research to determine the extent of information security vulnerabilities, developing and revising performance indicators, and evaluating security policies and practices.

The activities conducted by NIST in accordance with the Act are ongoing. For a comprehensive list of activities completed by NIST in FY 2014 as required by the Act, please see NIST's website at: *http://csrc.nist.gov/*. Additionally, as required by Section 303, NIST prepares an annual report on activities undertaken in the previous year. A copy of the most recent NIST Computer Security Division Annual Report is available online at: *http://csrc.nist.gov/publications/PubsTC.html*.

APPENDIX 2: SECURITY INCIDENTS BY CFO ACT AGENCY

The charts in this appendix illustrate a breakdown of the types of security incidents reported by each CFO Act Agency. The definitions that are used are the same as those utilized in Section II, however they have been relisted here for ease of access.

Table 16: US-CERT FY 2014 Incident Definitions

Category/Subcategories	Definition
Denial of Service (DoS)	This category is used for all *successful* DoS attacks, such as a flood of traffic which renders a web server unavailable to legitimate users.
Improper Usage	Improper Usage categorizes all incidents where a user violates acceptable computing policies or rules of behavior. These include incidents like the spillage of information from one classification level to another.
-Unauthorized Access	Unauthorized Access is when individual gains logical or physical access without permission to a Federal agency network, system, application, data or other resource. (*Subcategory of Improper Usage Category*)
-Social Engineering	Social Engineering is used to categorize fraudulent web sites and other attempts to entice users to provide sensitive information or download malicious code. Phishing is a set of Social Engineering, which is itself a subcategory of Unauthorized Access. (*Set of Unauthorized Access Subcategory*)
-Phishing	Phishing is an attempt by an individual or group to solicit personal information from unsuspecting users by employing social engineering techniques, typically via emails containing links to fraudulent websites. (*Set of Social Engineering Subcategory*)
-Equipment	This set of Unauthorized Access is used for all incidents involving lost, stolen or confiscated equipment, including mobile devices, laptops, backup disks or removable media. (*Set of Unauthorized Access Subcategory*)
-Policy Violation	Policy Violation is primarily used to categorize incidents of mishandling data in storage or transit, such as digital PII records or procurement sensitive information found unsecured or PII being emailed without proper encryption. (*Subcategory of Improper Usage Category*)
Malicious Code	Used for all *successful* executions or installations of malicious software which are not immediately quarantined and cleaned by preventative measures such as antivirus tools.
Non Cyber	Non Cyber is used for filing all reports of PII spillages or possible mishandling of PII which involve hard copies or printed material as opposed to digital records.
Other	For the purposes of this report, a separate superset of multiple subcategories has been employed to accommodate several low-frequency types of incident reports, such as unconfirmed third-party notifications, failed brute force attempts, port scans, or reported incidents where the cause is unknown.
Suspicious Network Activity	This category is primarily utilized for incident reports and notifications created from EINSTEIN data analyzed by US-CERT.

Source: Classifications and definitions provided by US-CERT

Figure 5: Security Incidents Reported - Department of Agriculture

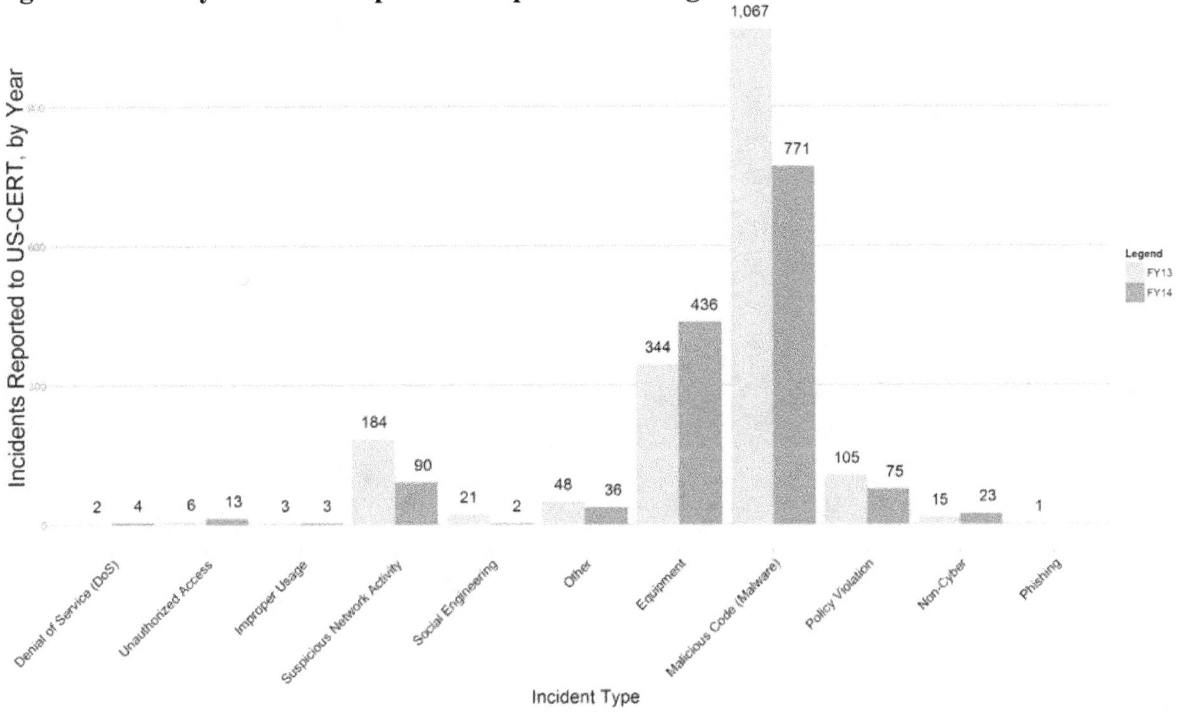

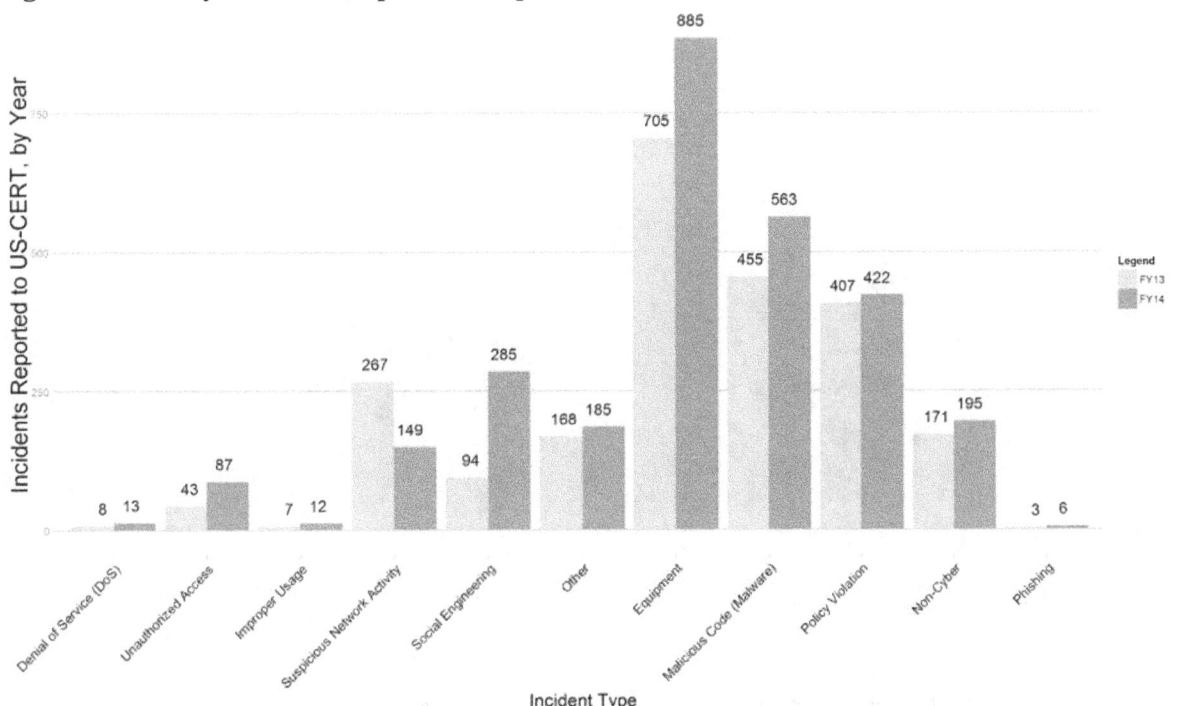

Source: Data reported to US-CERT Incident Reporting System from October 1, 2012, to September 30, 2014.

Figure 6: Security Incidents Reported - Department of Commerce

Source: Data reported to US-CERT Incident Reporting System from October 1, 2012, to September 30, 2014.

Figure 7: Security Incidents Reported - Department of Defense

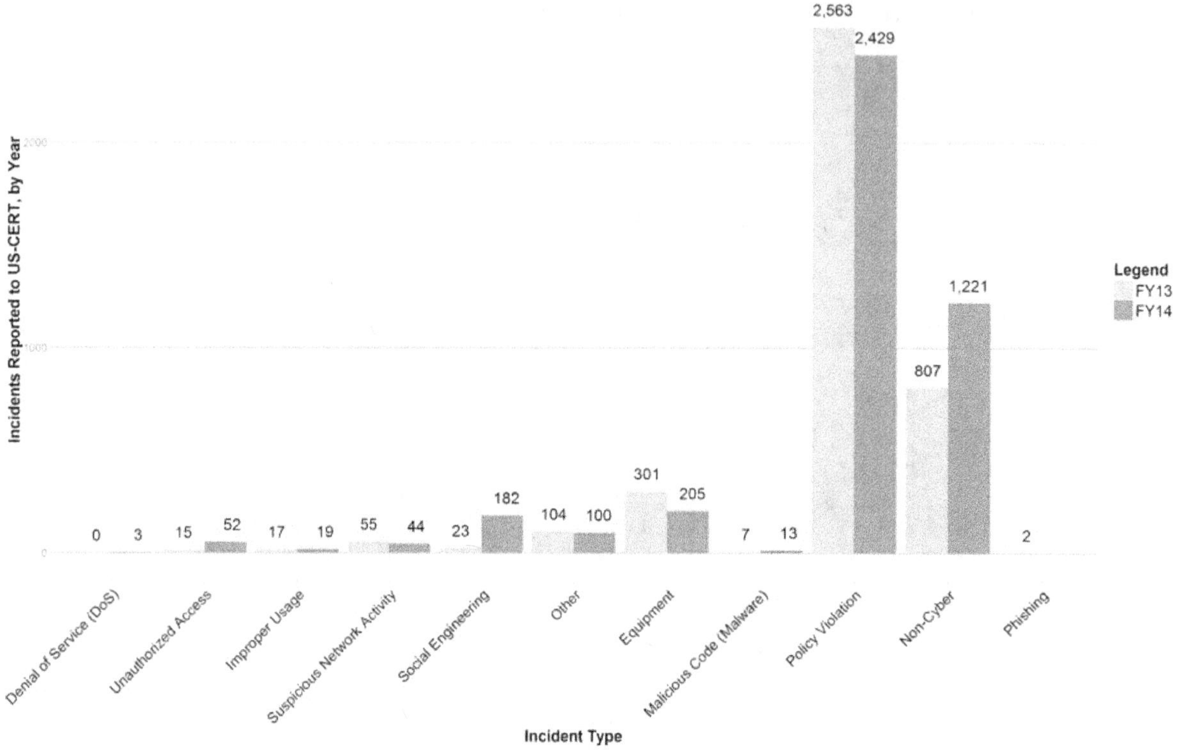

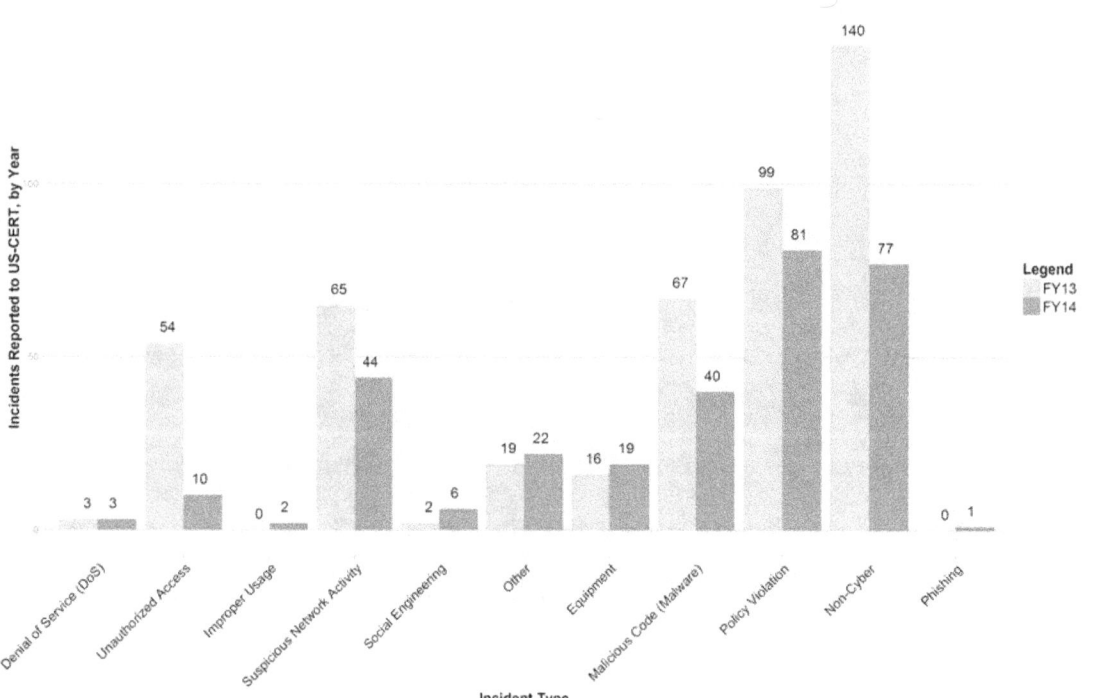

Source: Data reported to US-CERT Incident Reporting System from October 1, 2012, to September 30, 2014.

Figure 8: Security Incidents Reported - Department of Education

Source: Data reported to US-CERT Incident Reporting System from October 1, 2012, to September 30, 2014.

Figure 9: Security Incidents Reported - Department of Energy

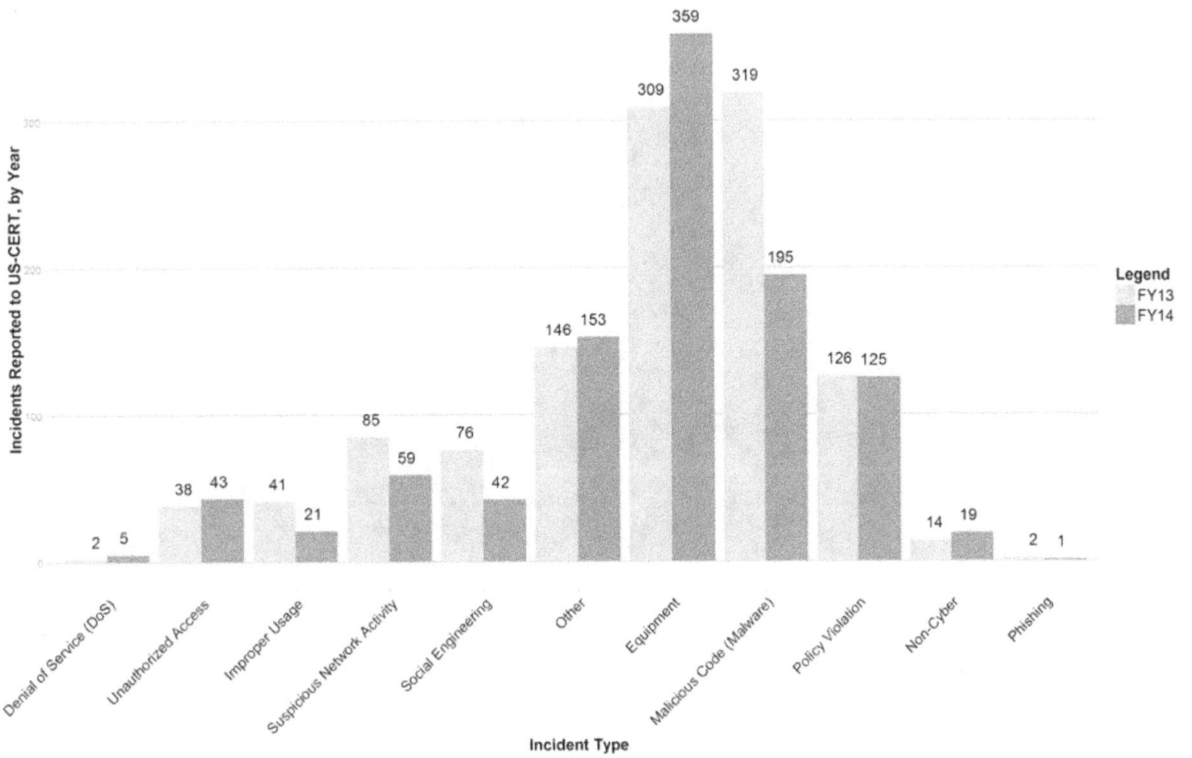

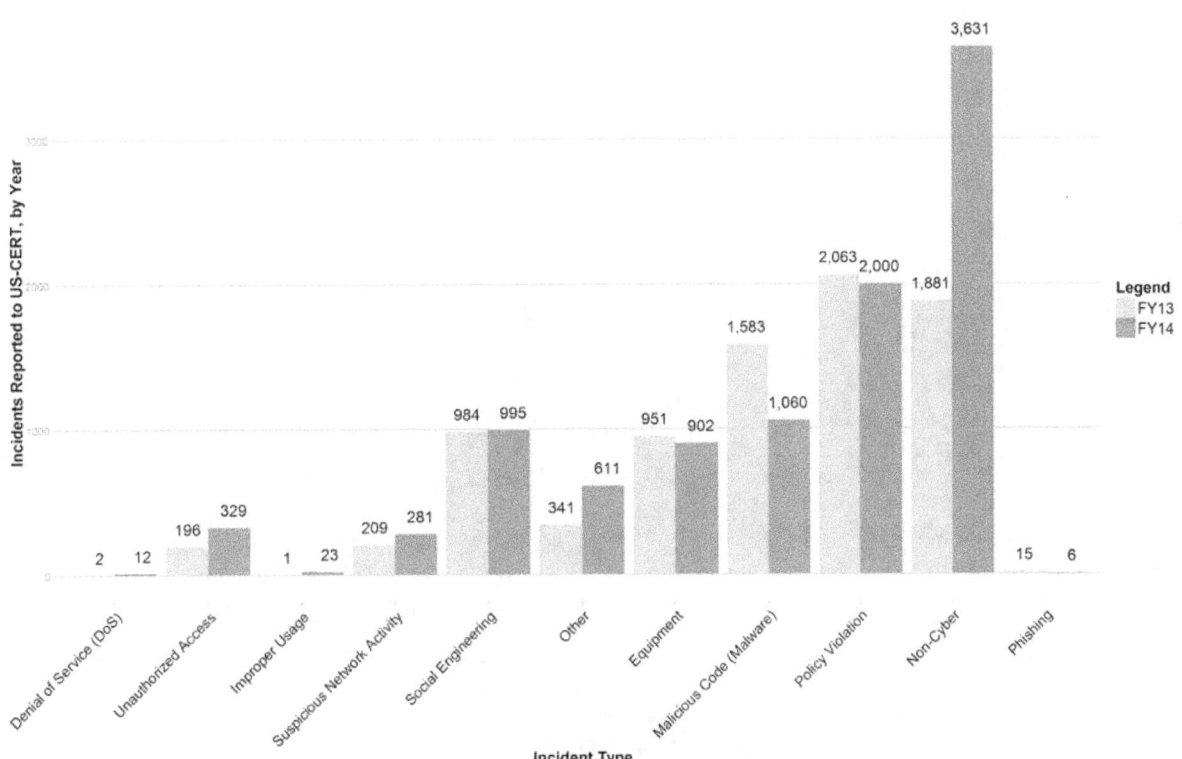

Source: Data reported to US-CERT Incident Reporting System from October 1, 2012, to September 30, 2014.

Figure 10: Security Incidents Reported - Department of Health and Human Services

Source: Data reported to US-CERT Incident Reporting System from October 1, 2012, to September 30, 2014.

Figure 11: Security Incidents Reported - Department of Homeland Security

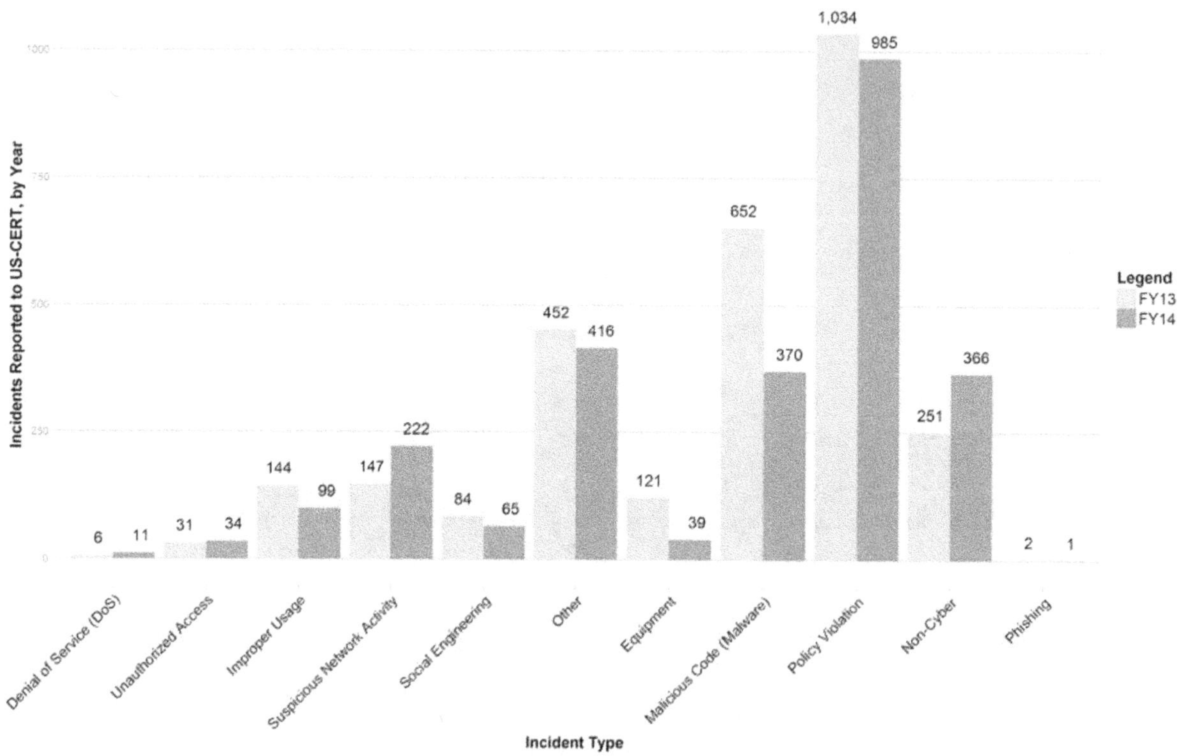

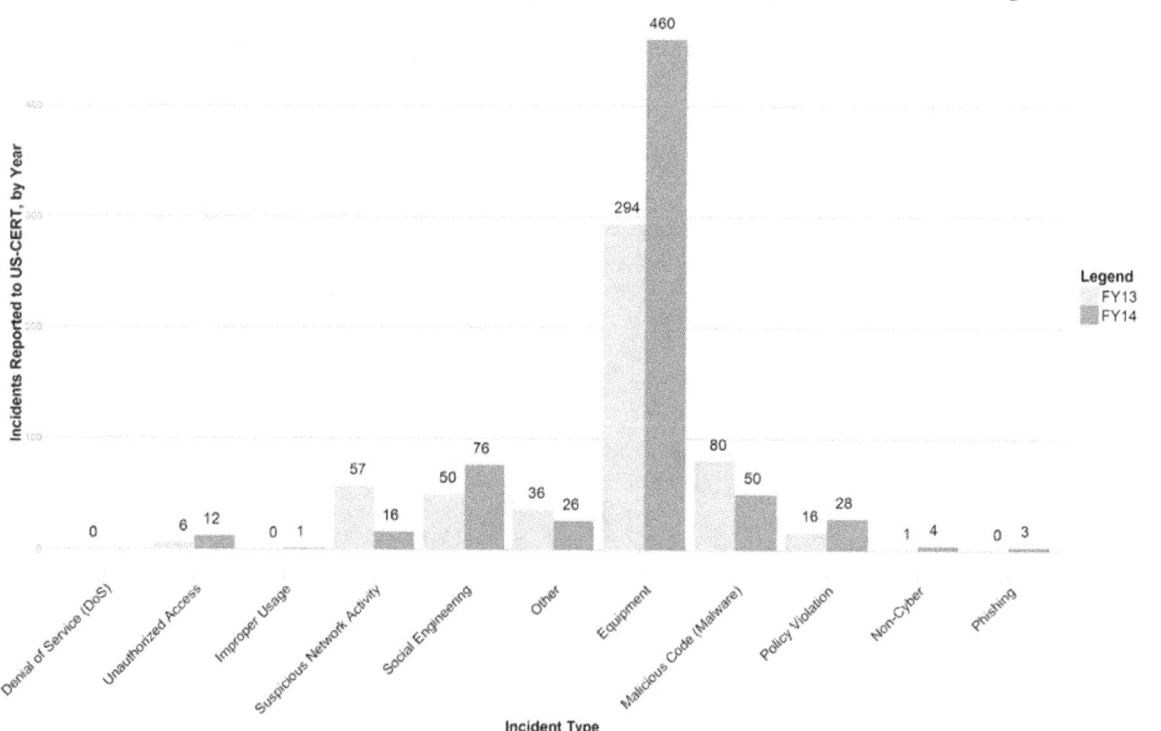

Source: Data reported to US-CERT Incident Reporting System from October 1, 2012, to September 30, 2014.

Figure 12: Security Incidents Reported - Department of Housing and Urban Development

Source: Data reported to US-CERT Incident Reporting System from October 1, 2012, to September 30, 2014.

Figure 13: Security Incidents Reported - Department of the Interior

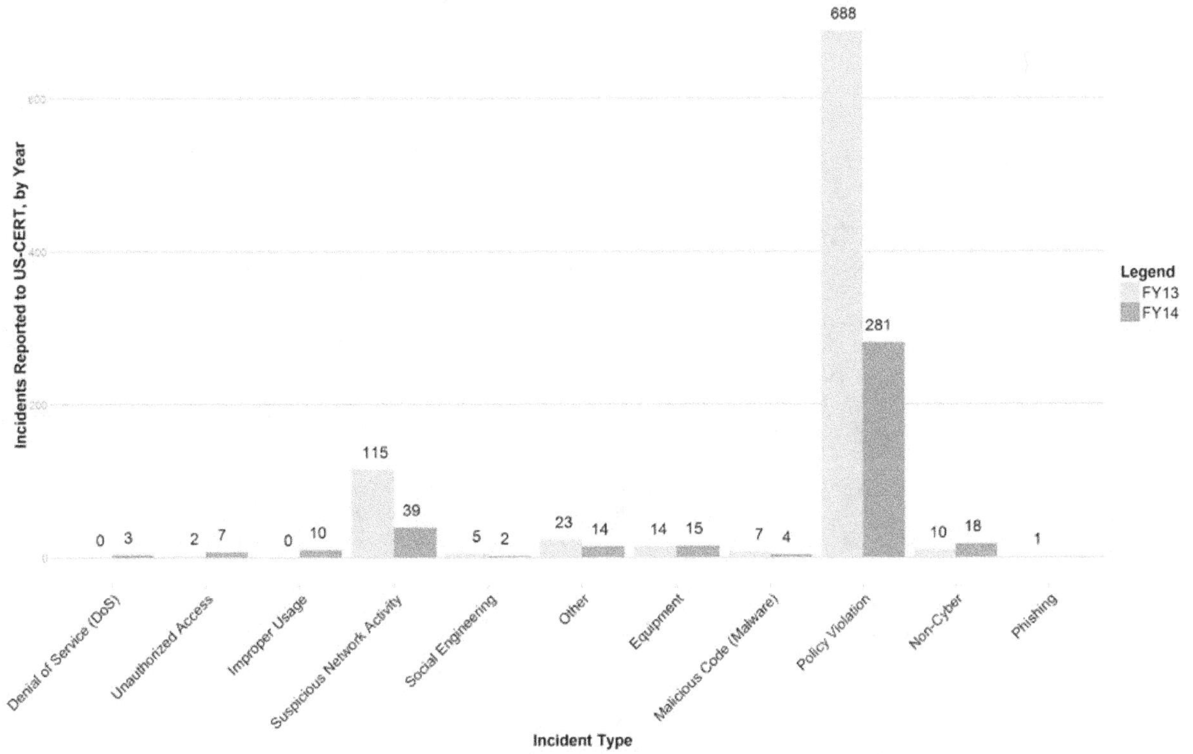

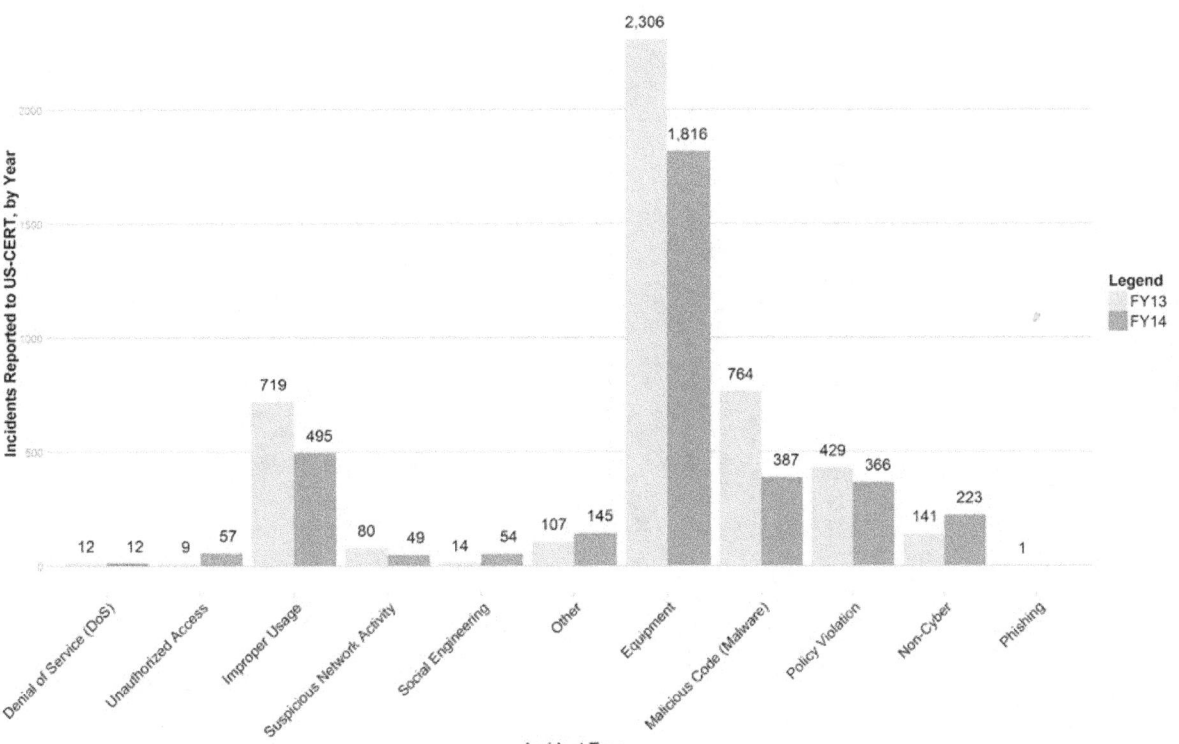

Source: Data reported to US-CERT Incident Reporting System from October 1, 2012, to September 30, 2014.

Figure 14: Security Incidents Reported - Department of Justice

Source: Data reported to US-CERT Incident Reporting System from October 1, 2012, to September 30, 2014.

Figure 15: Security Incidents Reported - Department of Labor

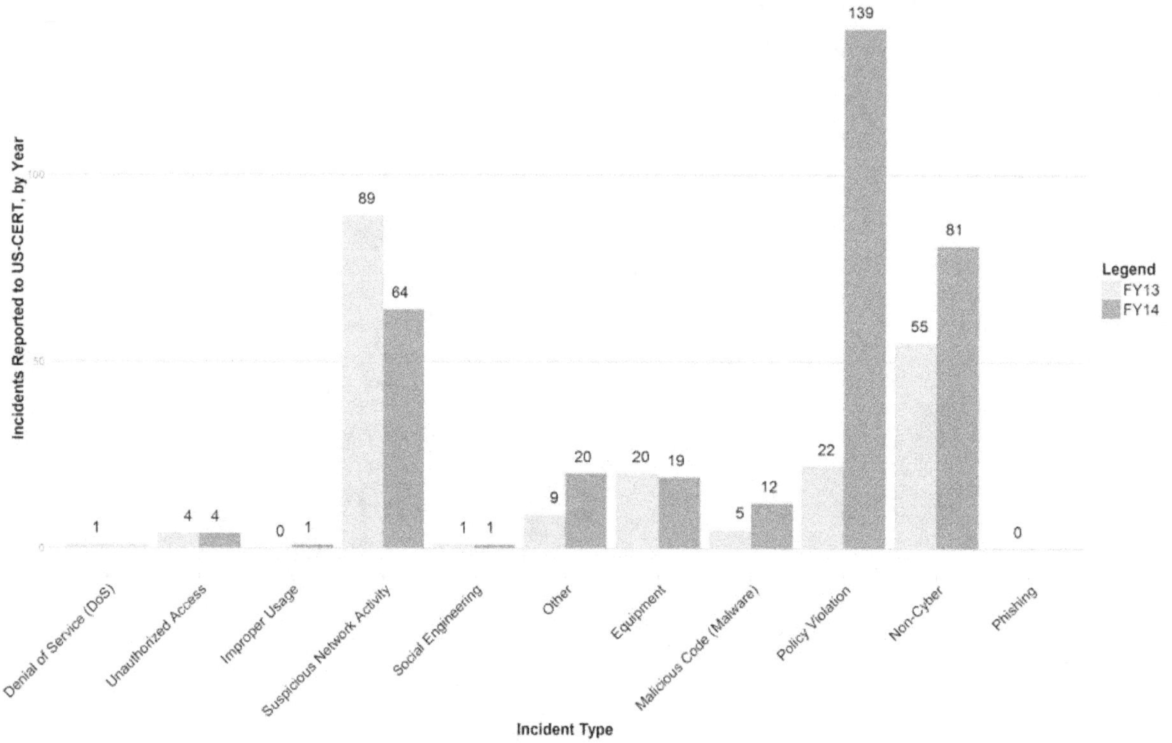

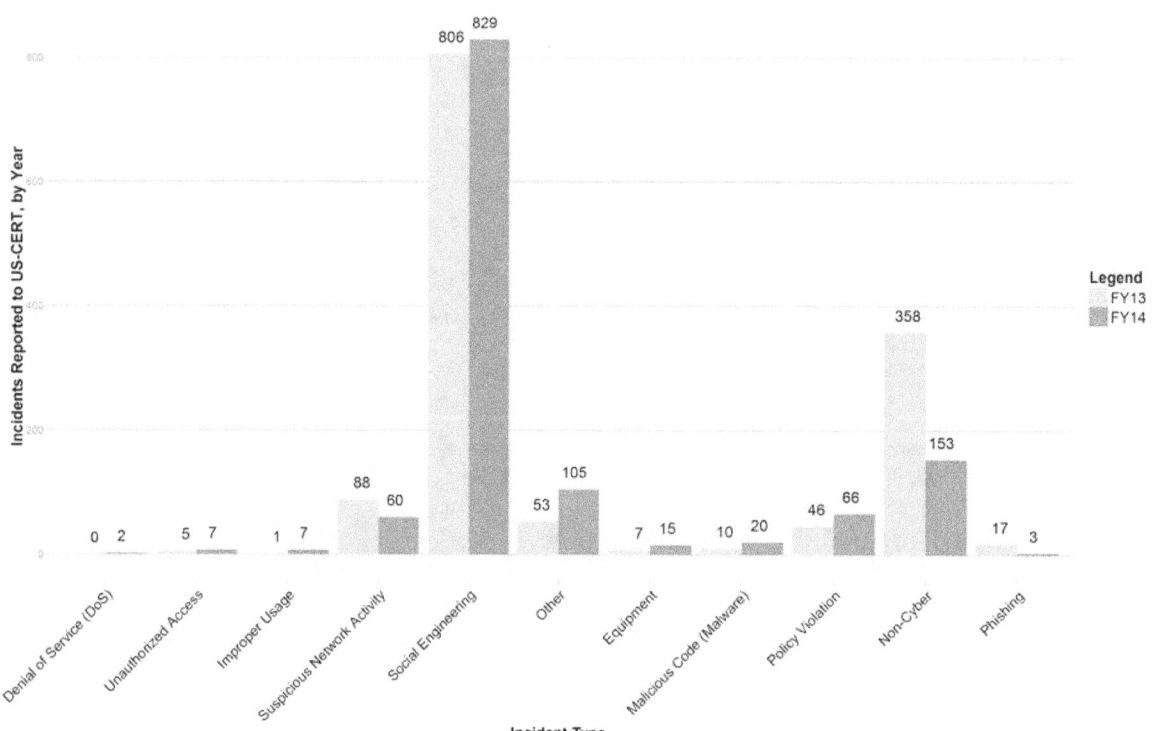

Source: Data reported to US-CERT Incident Reporting System from October 1, 2012, to September 30, 2014.

Figure 16: Security Incidents Reported - Department of State

Source: Data reported to US-CERT Incident Reporting System from October 1, 2012, to September 30, 2014.

Figure 17: Security Incidents Reported - Department of the Treasury

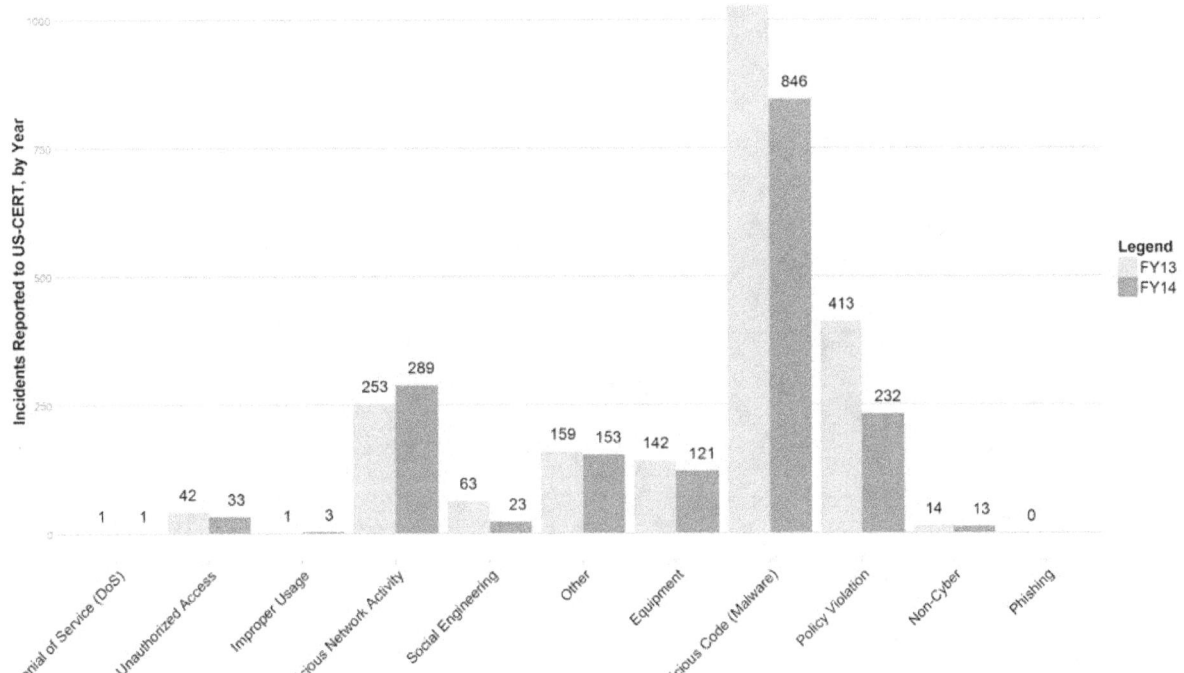

Source: Data reported to US-CERT Incident Reporting System from October 1, 2012, to September 30, 2014.

Figure 18: Security Incidents Reported - Department of Transportation

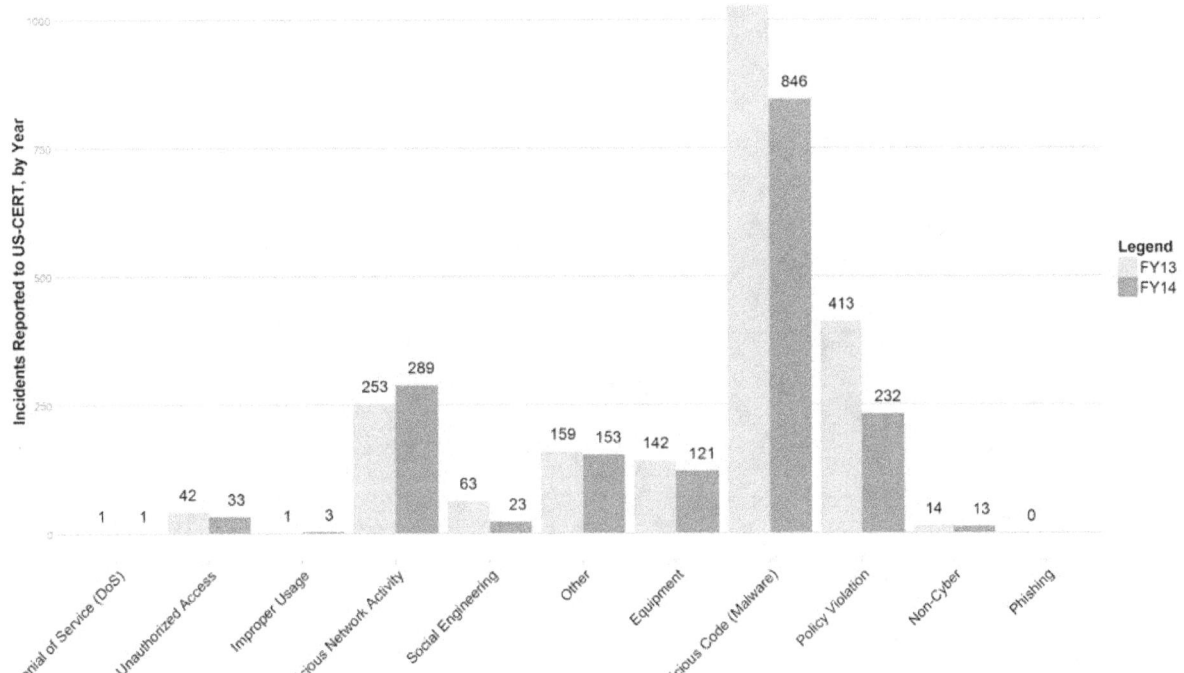

Source: Data reported to US-CERT Incident Reporting System from October 1, 2012, to September 30, 2014.

Figure 19: Security Incidents Reported - Department of Veterans Affairs

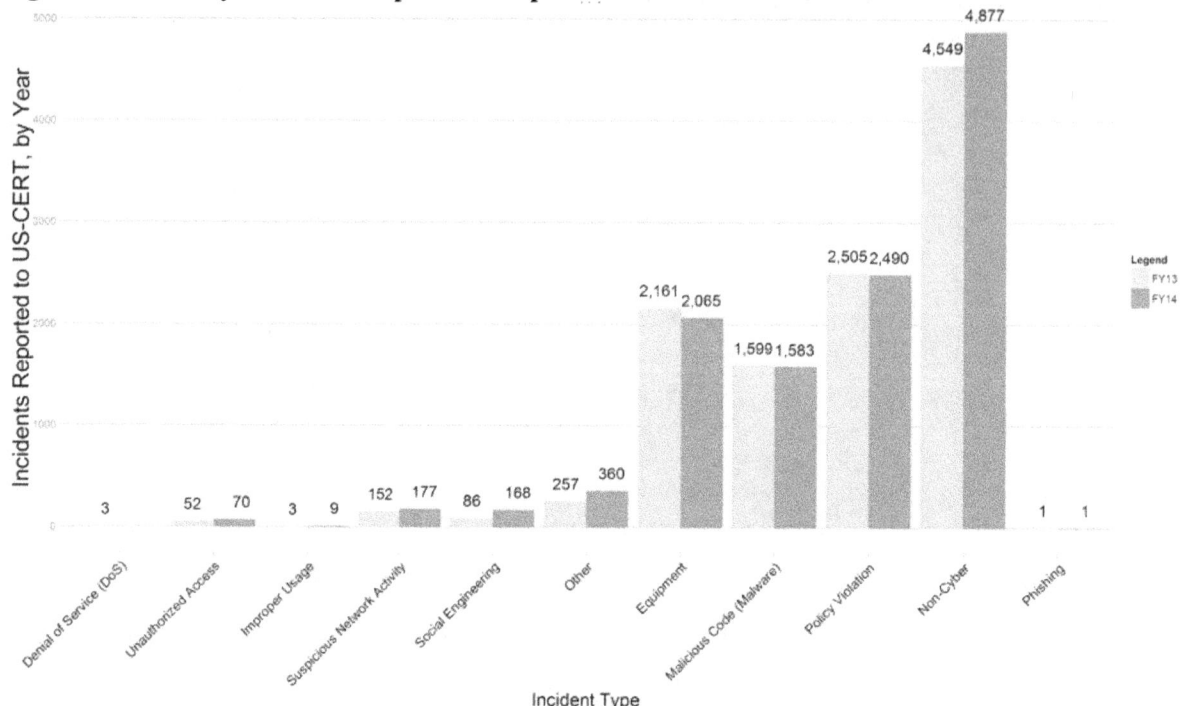

Source: Data reported to US-CERT Incident Reporting System from October 1, 2012, to September 30, 2014.

Figure 20: Security Incidents Reported - Environmental Protection Agency

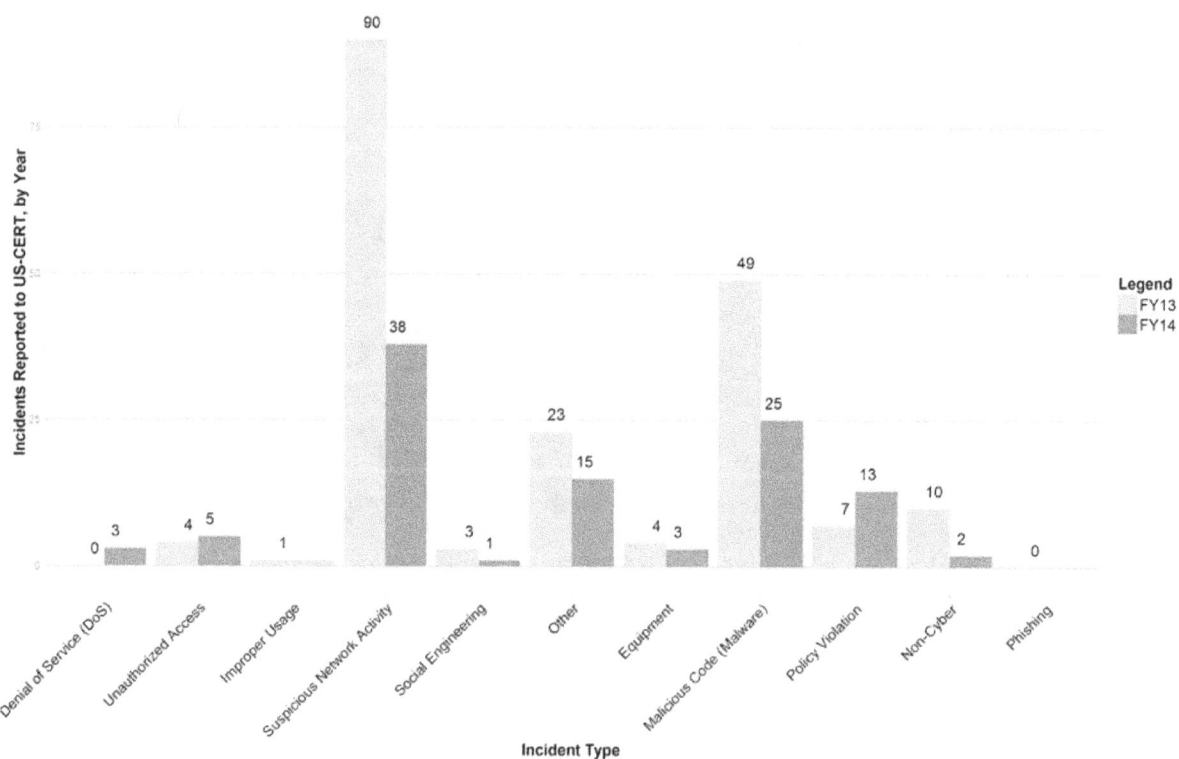

Source: Data reported to US-CERT Incident Reporting System from October 1, 2012, to September 30, 2014.

Figure 21: Security Incidents Reported - General Services Administration

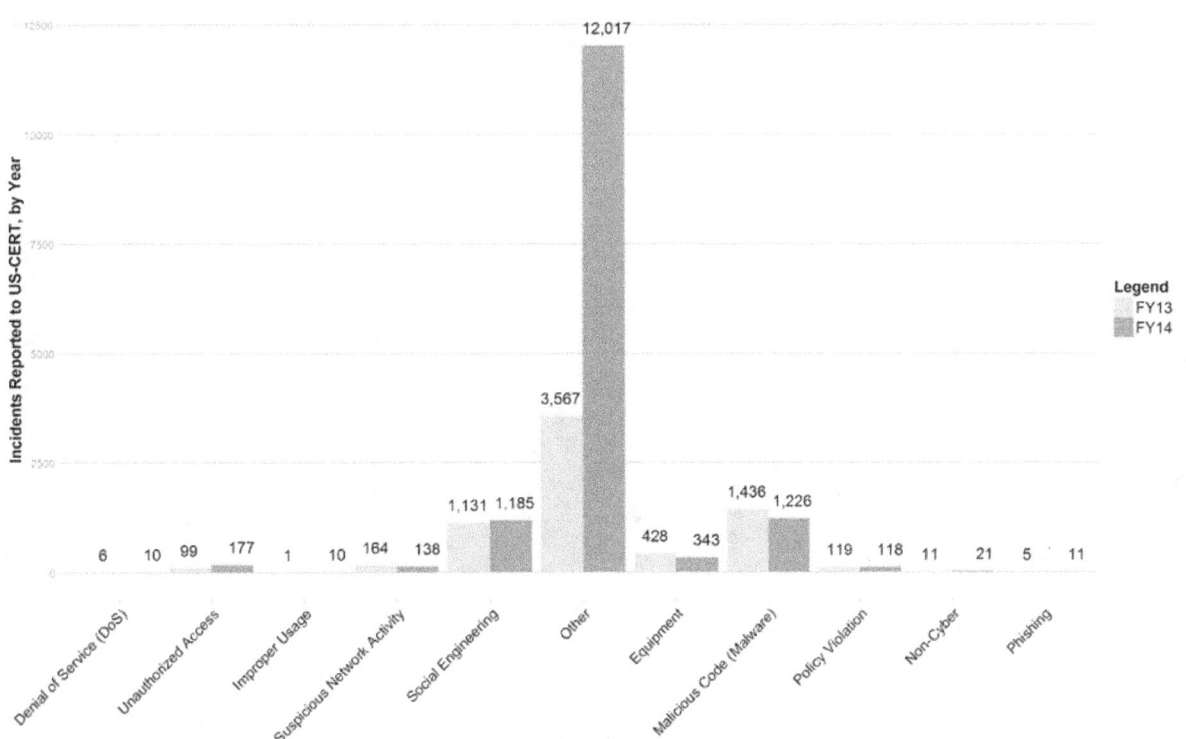

Source: Data reported to US-CERT Incident Reporting System from October 1, 2012, to September 30, 2014.

Figure 22: Security Incidents Reported - National Aeronautics and Space Administration

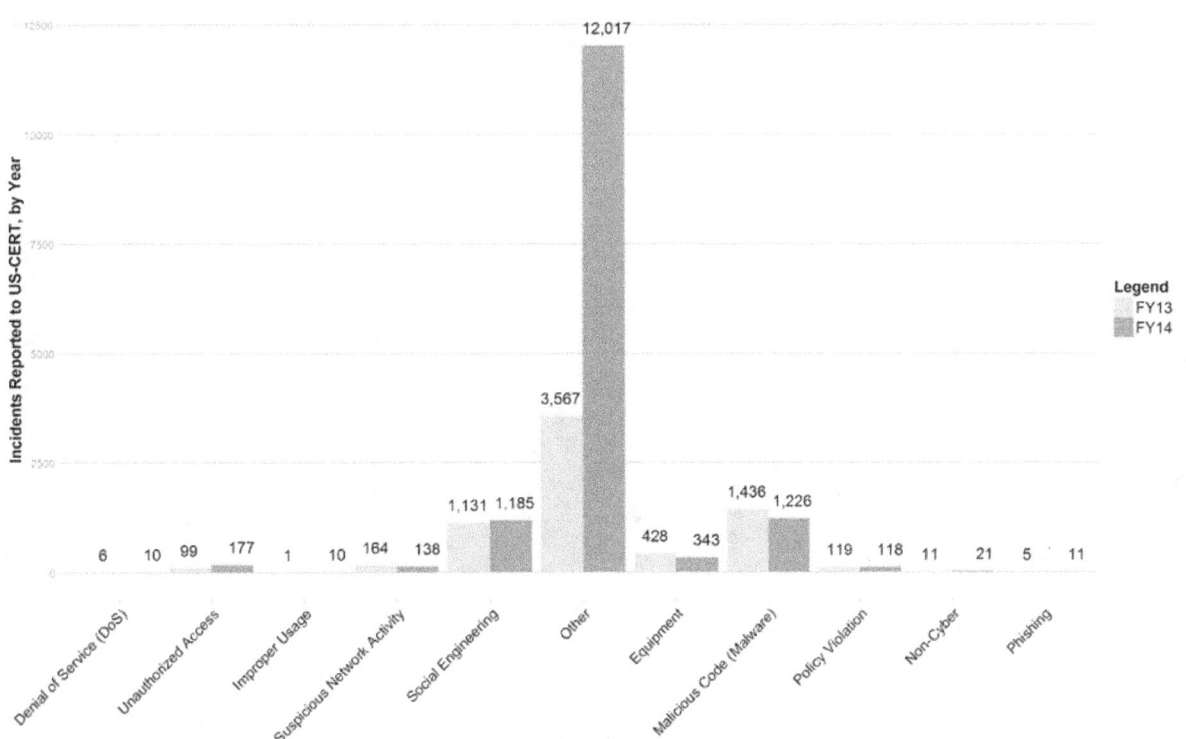

Source: Data reported to US-CERT Incident Reporting System from October 1, 2012, to September 30, 2014.

Figure 23: Security Incidents Reported - National Science Foundation

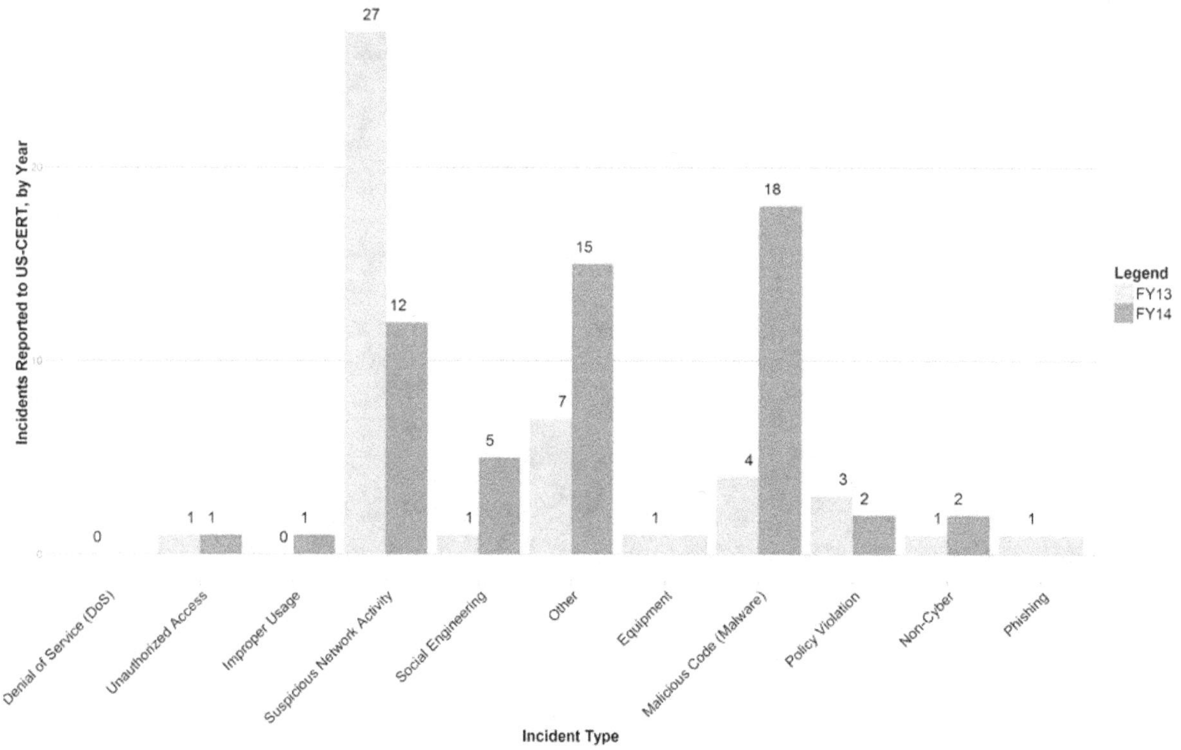

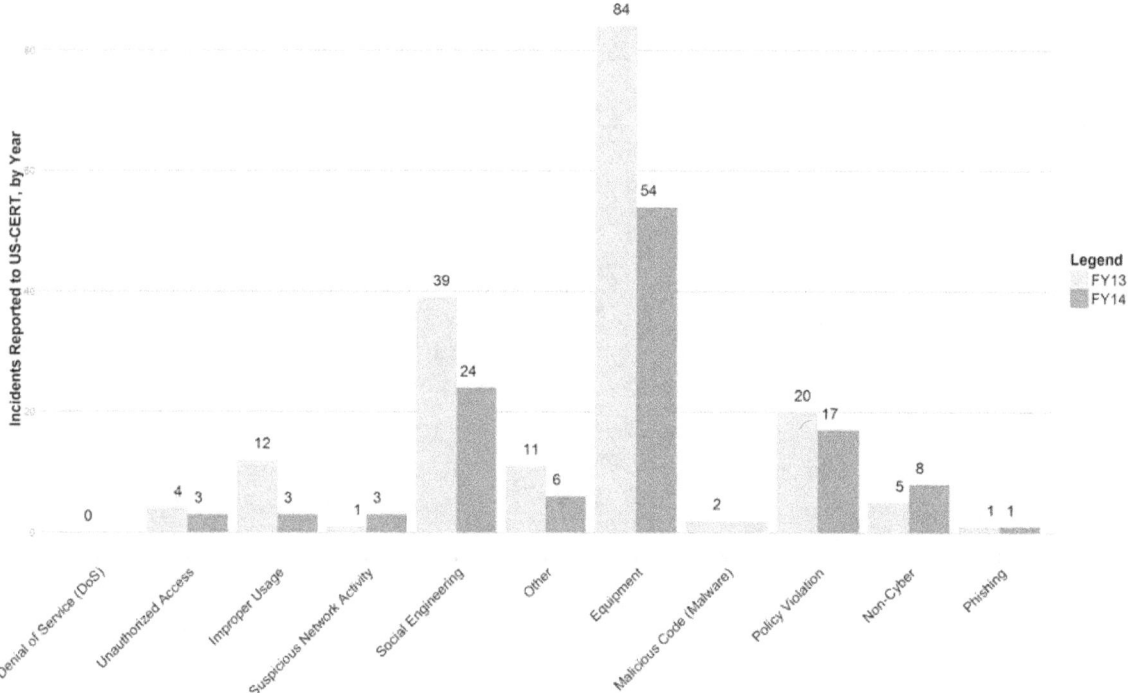

Source: Data reported to US-CERT Incident Reporting System from October 1, 2012, to September 30, 2014.

Figure 24: Security Incidents Reported - Nuclear Regulatory Commission

Source: Data reported to US-CERT Incident Reporting System from October 1, 2012, to September 30, 2014.

Figure 25: Security Incidents Reported - Office of Personnel Management

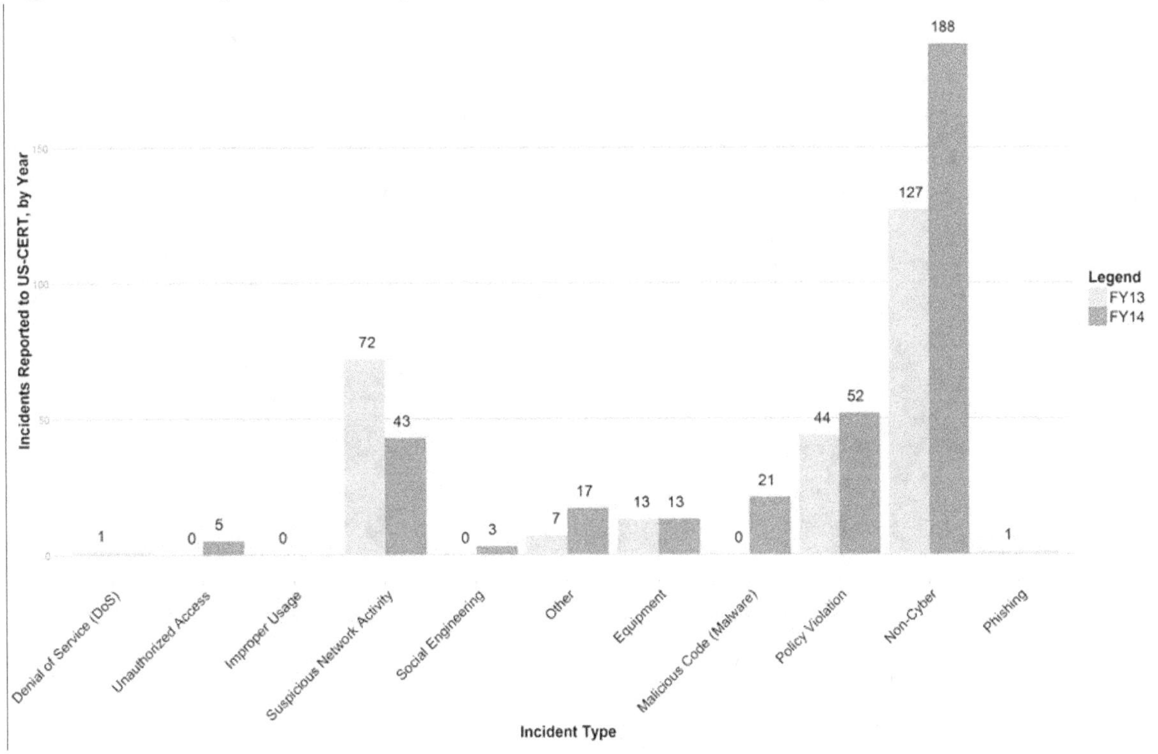

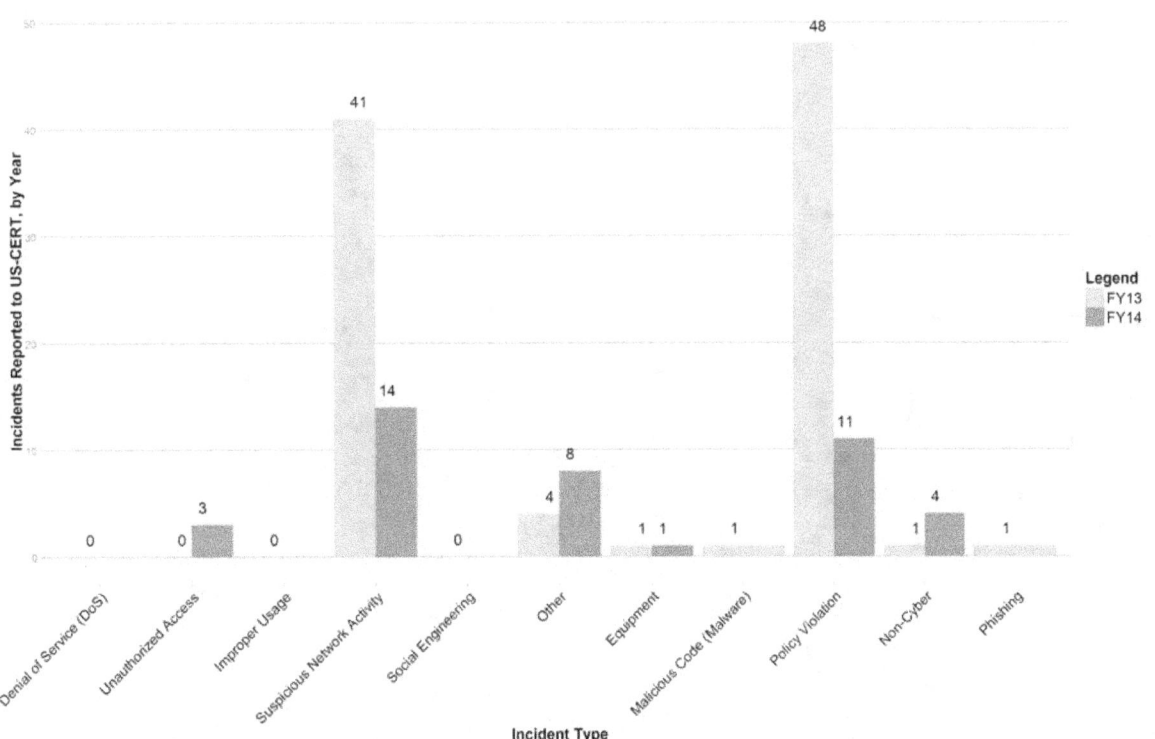

Source: Data reported to US-CERT Incident Reporting System from October 1, 2012, to September 30, 2014.

Figure 26: Security Incidents Reported - Small Business Administration

Source: Data reported to US-CERT Incident Reporting System from October 1, 2012, to September 30, 2014.

Figure 27: Security Incidents Reported - Social Security Administration

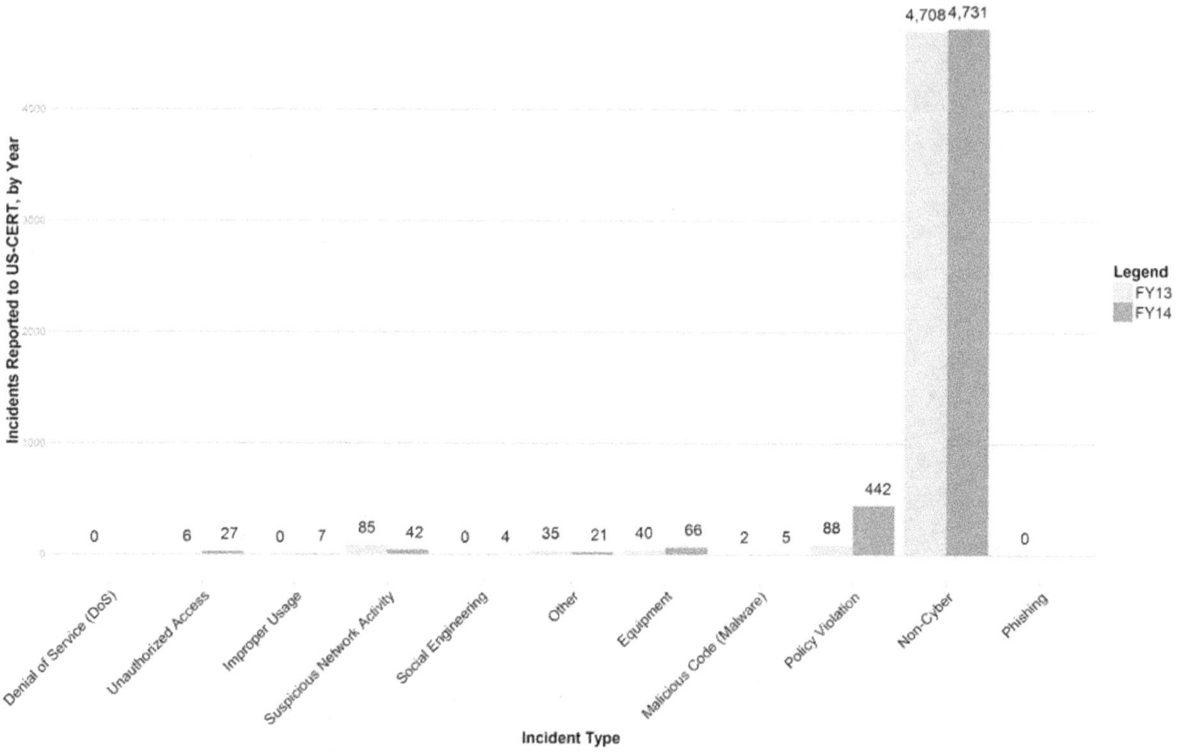

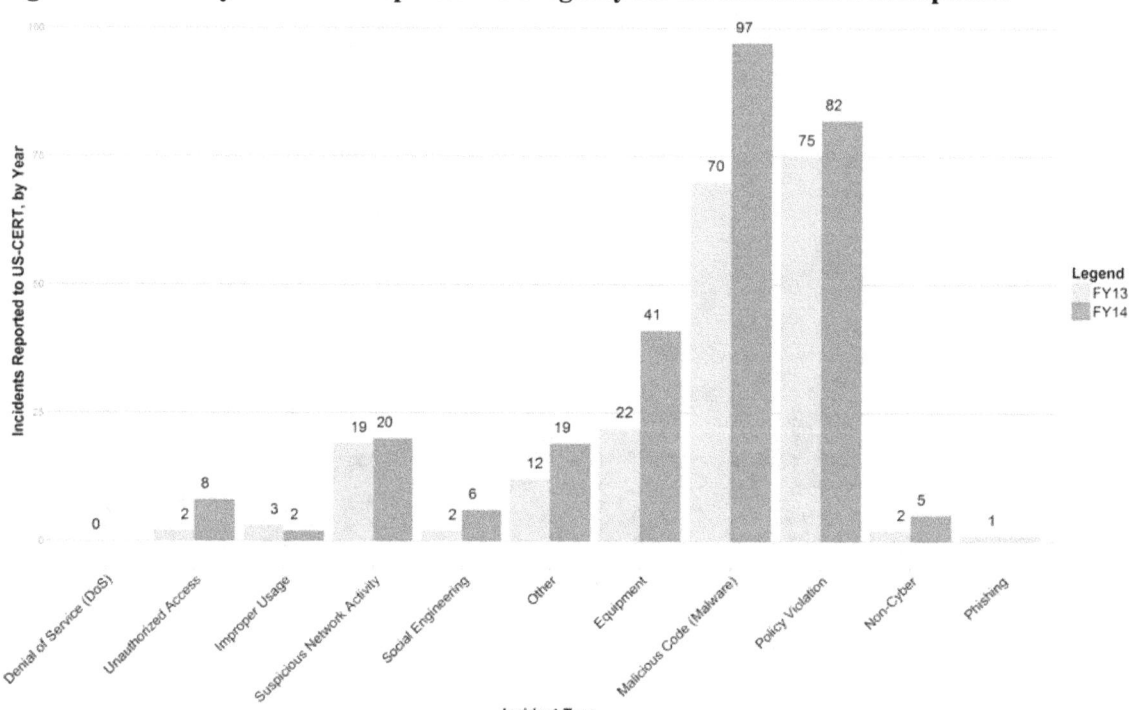

Source: Data reported to US-CERT Incident Reporting System from October 1, 2012, to September 30, 2014.

Figure 28: Security Incidents Reported - US Agency for International Development

Source: Data reported to US-CERT Incident Reporting System from October 1, 2012, to September 30, 2014

APPENDIX 3: FY 2014 CAP & KEY FISMA METRICS DETAILS

This Appendix identifies both CAP goal information as well as KFMs related to the priority areas described in Section II, which represent the basic building blocks of a strong cybersecurity incident mitigation posture. More specific information on each of these metrics is also available online at the *DHS FY 2014 CIO Annual FISMA Metrics page*. **Table 17** below summarizes the four cybersecurity priority areas, the metrics and definitions used to track progress, and CFO Act Agency performance on these metrics in 2014. The agencies reporting the lowest scores for each metric have also been identified. **Table 30** summarizes the same metrics for the Non-CFO Act, small and micro agencies.

Table 17: CAP Goal and Key FISMA Metrics (KFMs), Definitions, Sources, and CFO Act Agency Performance FY 2014

Key performance area	Sub-performance area	Definition	Source	CFO Act Agency Performance Average	Lowest Scoring Agencies
Information Security Continuous Monitoring (ISCM)	Information Security Continuous Monitoring (ISCM) CAP Goal	The average of automated asset, configuration, and vulnerability management. The average is weighted by the total number of the organization's hardware assets connected to the organization's unclassified network(s).	FISMA Agency Level Questions Data (Questions 2.1, 2.2, and 4.1), and FISMA Agency Level Secure Configuration Management Assets and Percentage Data (Questions 3.1.2 and 3.1.3) reported to DHS via CyberScope from October 1, 2013, to September 30, 2014.	92%	HHS (80%) EPA (82%) DOT (88%)
	Automated Asset Management (ISCM) CAP Goal	Percentage of assets where an automated capability (device discovery process) provides visibility at the organization's enterprise level into asset inventory information for all hardware assets. The average is weighted by the total number of the organization's hardware assets connected to the organization's unclassified network(s).	FISMA Agency Level Questions Data (Questions 2.1 and 2.2) reported to DHS via CyberScope from October 1, 2013, to September 30, 2014.	96%	EPA (76%) USAID (85%) Commerce (86%)

FEDERAL INFORMATION SECURITY MANAGEMENT ACT

Key performance area	Sub-performance area	Definition	Source	CFO Act Agency Performance Average	Lowest Scoring Agencies
	Automated Asset Management: Detect and Block Unauthorized Software (KFM)	Percentage of applicable assets for which the organization has implemented an automated capability to detect and block unauthorized software from executing or for which no such software exists for the device type. The average is weighted by the total number of the organization's hardware assets connected to the organization's unclassified network(s).	FISMA Agency Level Questions Data (Question 2.1 and 2.5) reported to DHS via CyberScope from October 1, 2013, to September 30, 2014.	69%	NASA (0%) VA (0%) Treasury (36%)
	Automated Configuration Management (ISCM) CAP Goal	Percentage of the applicable hardware assets of each kind of operating system software that has an automated capability to identify deviations from the approved configuration baselines and provide visibility at the organization's enterprise level. The average is weighted by the total number of the organization's hardware assets connected to the organization's unclassified network(s).	FISMA Agency Level Secure Configuration Management Assets and Percentage Data (Questions 3.1.2 and 3.1.3) reported to DHS via CyberScope from October 1, 2013, to September 30, 2014.	86%	HHS (69%) DOD (77%) Interior (86%)

Key performance area	Sub-performance area	Definition	Source	CFO Act Agency Performance Average	Lowest Scoring Agencies
	Automated Vulnerability Management (ISCM) CAP Goal	Percentage of hardware assets that are evaluated using an automated capability that identifies NIST National Vulnerability Database vulnerabilities (CVEs) present with visibility at the organization's enterprise level. The average is weighted by the total number of the organization's hardware assets connected to the organization's unclassified network(s).	FISMA Agency Level Questions Data (Questions 2.1 & 4.1) reported to DHS via CyberScope from October 1, 2013, to September 30, 2014.	94%	EPA (74%) HHS (77%) DOT (77%)
Strong Authentication and Data Protection	Strong Authentication CAP Goal	Percentage of all people required to use Personal Identity Verfication (PIV) to authenticate. The average is weighted by the total number of people at the organization who have network accounts.	FISMA Agency Level Questions Data (Questions 5.1, 5.2.5, 5.3 & 5.4.5) reported to DHS via CyberScope from October 1, 2013, to September 30, 2014.	72%	SBA, NRC, HUD, Labor, and State, all at 0%

Key performance area	Sub-performance area	Definition	Source	CFO Act Agency Performance Average	Lowest Scoring Agencies
	Remote Access Authentication (KFM)	Percentage of people who are required to log on to the organization's remote access solution(s) to obtain access to the organization's LAN/WAN resources or services using a two-factor PIV card as the nromal mode of authentication for remote access. The average is weighted by the total number of people at the organization who log onto the organization's remote access solution(s) to obtain access to the organization's desktop LAN/WAN resources or services.	FISMA Agency Level Questions Data (Questions 5. 10 and 5.11.5) reported to DHS via CyberScope from October 1, 2013, to September 30, 2014.	77%	HUD (0%) State (0%) DOT (1%)
	Remote Access Encryption: FIPS 140-2 validated cryptographic modules (KFM)	Percentage of remote access connections that utilize FIPS 140-2 validated cryptographic modules.	FISMA Agency Level Questions Data (Question 5.12.1) reported to DHS via CyberScope from October 1, 2013, to September 30, 2014.	96%	SBA (50%) NASA (53%) HHS (95%)

Key performance area	Sub-performance area	Definition	Source	CFO Act Agency Performance Average	Lowest Scoring Agencies
	Remote Access Encryption: Prohibits split tunneling (KFM)	Percentage of remote access connections that prohibit split tunneling and/or dual connected remote hosts where the laptop has two active connections.	FISMA Agency Level Questions Data (Question 5.12.2) reported to DHS via CyberScope from October 1, 2013, to September 30, 2014.	75%	USAID (0%) State (0%) EPA (15%)
	Remote Access Encryption: Time-out after 30 minutes of inactivity (KFM)	Percentage of remote access connections that are configured in accordance with OMB M-07-16 to time-out after 30 minutes of inactivity (or less) and require re-authentication to reestablish session.	FISMA Agency Level Questions Data (Question 5.12.3) reported to DHS via CyberScope from October 1, 2013, to September 30, 2014.	83%	OPM (0%) USAID (0%) DOT (30%)
	Remote Access Encryption: Scans for malware (KFM)	Percentage of remote access connections that scan for malware upon connection.	FISMA Agency Level Questions Data (Question 5.12.4) reported to DHS via CyberScope from October 1, 2013, to September 30, 2014.	42%	OPM, NSF, GSA, EPA, State, and ED all 0%
	Data Protection: Mobile Asset Encryption (KFM)	Percentage of mobile assets with encryption of data on the device. The average is weighted by the total number of mobile assets at the organization.	FISMA Agency Level Questions Data (Questions 6.1.1-6.1.2.5) reported to DHS via CyberScope from October 1, 2013, to September 30, 2014.	55%	VA (5%) NRC (41%) Energy (55%)

FEDERAL INFORMATION SECURITY MANAGEMENT ACT

Key performance area	Sub-performance area	Definition	Source	CFO Act Agency Performance Average	Lowest Scoring Agencies
	Data Protection: Anti-spoofing (KFM)	Percentage of email systems implementing anti-spoofing technoligies when sending messages, and when receiving messages.	Sending: FISMA Agency Level Questions Data (Questions 6.2.1) Receiving: FISMA Agency Level Questions Data (Questions 6.2.2) reported to DHS via CyberScope from October 1, 2013, to September 30, 2014.	Sending: 79% Receiving: 87%	Sending: EPA, USAID, ED (0%) Receiving: EPA (0%), VA (0%), DOT (50%)
	Data Protection: Quarantine maliciouios payload (KFM)	Percentage of email traffic that is on systems that have the capability to analyze links or attachmetns to identify and quarantine suspected malicious payload (when receiving messages).	FISMA Agency Level Questions Data (Questions 6.2.3) reported to DHS via CyberScope from October 1, 2013, to September 30, 2014.	90%	NASA (0%) DOT (50%) Justice (60%)
	Data Protection: Digitially signed email (KFM)	Percentage of email traffic that is on systems that have the capability to digitially sign email (when sending messages).	FISMA Agency Level Questions Data (Questions 6.2.4) reported to DHS via CyberScope from October 1, 2013, to September 30, 2014.	56%	SBA, Interior, State, Labor, HUD, and USDA all 0%
	Data Protection: Encryption of Email (KFM)	Percentage of email traffic that is on systems that have FIPS 140-2 Encryption of Email (when sending messages).	FISMA Agency Level Questions Data (Questions 6.2.5) reported to DHS via CyberScope from October 1, 2013, to September 30, 2014.	54%	SBA, NSF, DOT , State, Labor, and USDA all 0%

Key performance area	Sub-performance area	Definition	Source	CFO Act Agency Performance Average	Lowest Scoring Agencies
	TIC 2.0 Capabilities CAP Goal	Percentage of the required TIC 2.0 Capabilities implemented.	FISMA Agency Level Questions Data (Questions 7.1) reported to DHS via CyberScope from October 1, 2013, to September 30, 2014.	92%	HHS (74%) Commerce (75%) OPM (77%)
Boundary Protection	TIC Traffic Consolidation CAP Goal	Percentage of external network traffic to/from the organization's networks that passes through a TIC/MTIPS.	FISMA Agency Level Questions Data (Questions 7.2) reported to DHS via CyberScope from October 1, 2013, to September 30, 2014.	95%	VA (57%) Energy (72%) Commerce (86%)
	DNSSEC Enabled Domains	Percentage of domains, out of the number tested that were found to be Operational (green), which refers to functional states based on NIST determined characteristics	National Institute of Standards and Technology (NIST) data on Estimating DNSSEC External Service Deployment Status on September 30, 2014.	92%	DOD (36%) Energy (52%) Justice (92%)

Key performance area	Sub-performance area	Definition	Source	CFO Act Agency Performance Average	Lowest Scoring Agencies
Training and Education	Security Training (KFM)	Percentage of the organization's network users who were given and successfully completed cybersecurity awareness training in the past year (at least annually). The average is weighted by the total number of people at the organization who have network accounts. & Percentage of the organizations network users and other staff who have significant security responsibilities and have taken security training within the organizational standard for the longest acceptable amount of time between security training events for personnel who have significant security responsibilities. The average is weighted by the total number of network users and other staff at the organization who have significant security responsibilities.	FISMA Agency Level Questions Data (Questions 5.1, 5.3 and 9.1) reported to DHS via CyberScope from October 1, 2013, to September 30, 2014. & FISMA Agency Level Questions Data (Questions 9.3 and 9.3.2 reported to DHS via CyberScope from October 1, 2013, to September 30, 2014.	93% 80%	USAID (80%), Treasury (88%), DHS (91%) NRC (29%), State (43%), USAID 58%

The sections following delve into performance on each metric outlined in **Table 17**, highlighting findings which are particularly pertinent in assessing the state of agency cybersecurity.

Information Security Continuous Monitoring (ISCM)

Asset Management

Organizations must first know about assets before they can manage them for configuration. Agencies report on the percentage of assets that are covered by an automated capability to provide visibility into inventory information. CFO Act Agency performance on this metric improved from 83% in FY 2013 to 96% in FY 2014. Fourteen agencies are at or above 95%. As can be seen in **Table 18** below, the agencies with the lowest percentage of assets covered by automated capability are EPA (76%), USAID (85%), and Commerce (86%).

Table 18: Automated Asset Management FY 2013 & FY 2014

Agency	Automated Asset Management FY 2013 (%)	Automated Asset Management FY 2014 (%)
EPA	39	76
USAID	95	85
Commerce	73	86
State	78	87
NRC	100	89
HUD	82	93
HHS	97	93
NASA	99	93
VA	67	94
Energy	86	94
OPM	95	95
DOT	57	96
DOD	81	97
Interior	94	98
Treasury	91	99
DHS	95	99
USDA	96	99
Justice	99	99
SBA	86	100
Labor	99	100
ED	100	100
GSA	100	100
NSF	100	100
SSA	100	100
CFO Act Agency Average*	83	96

*The average is weighted by the total number of the organization's hardware assets connected to the organization's unclassified network(s).
Source: Analysis of FISMA Agency Level Questions Data (Question 2.1 and 2.2), reported to DHS via CyberScope from October 1, 2012, to September 30, 2014.

As part of oversight of agency asset management practices, agencies report on the percentage of applicable assets for which the organization has implemented an automated capability to detect and block unauthorized software from executing, for which no software exists for the device type. **Table 19** below illustrates CFO act agency performance on this metric, with NASA (0%), VA (0%), and Treasury (36%) displaying the lowest percentages.

Table 19: Detect and Block Unauthorized Software

Agency	Assets with automated capability to detect and block software FY 2014 (%)
NASA	0
VA	0
Treasury	36
Commerce	50
DHS	51
USDA	54
HHS	55
Interior	55
ED	71
DOT	73
USAID	75
EPA	77
NSF	83
State	85
Energy	89
NRC	89
DOD	92
GSA	98
Labor	98
HUD	99
Justice	99
OPM	100
SBA	100
SSA	100
CFO Act Agency Average*	69

*The average is weighted by the total number of the organization's hardware assets connected to the organization's unclassified network(s).
Source: Analysis of FISMA Agency Level Questions Data (Questions 2.1 and 2.5), reported to DHS via CyberScope from October 1, 2013, to September 30, 2014.

Configuration Management

Configuration management defines the assets to which controls should apply. The goal of improved configuration management is to make assets harder to exploit. The configuration management capability needs to be accurate and complete, and operate in near-real time.

Agencies are asked for the percentage of applicable hardware assets which are covered by an automated capability to identify deviations from the approved configuration baseline. CFO Act Agency performance on this metric improved from 79% in FY 2013 to 86% in FY 2014. Fourteen agencies are at or above 95%. As can be seen in **Table 20** below, the lowest scoring agencies are HHS (69%), DOD (77%), Interior (86%), and DHS (86%).

Table 20: Automated Configuration Management FY 2013 & FY 2014

Agency	Automated Configuration Management FY 2013 (%)	Automated Configuration Management FY 2014 (%)
HHS	90	69
DOD	68	77
Interior	68	86
DHS	92	86
NSF	85	88
Commerce	61	89
DOT	46	90
NRC	90	91
Energy	88	92
SSA	94	94
HUD	86	95
EPA	95	95
GSA	95	95
ED	100	95
NASA	83	96
State	78	98
Treasury	87	99
Labor	95	99
Justice	100	99
SBA	2	100
OPM	100	100
USAID	100	100
USDA	100	100
VA	100	100
CFO Act Agency Average*	79	86

*The average is weighted by the total number of the organization's hardware assets connected to the organization's unclassified network(s).

Source: Analysis of FISMA Agency Level Secure Configuration Management Assets and Percentage Data (Questions 3.1.2 and 3.1.3) reported to DHS via CyberScope from October 1, 2012, to September 30, 2014.

Vulnerability Management

Unpatched vulnerabilities are a major attack vector. A key goal of vulnerability management is to make assets harder to exploit through mitigation or remediation of vulnerabilities identified in NIST's National Vulnerability Database. A key assumption is that vulnerability management covers the universe of applicable assets (defined under asset management).

Agencies report on the percentage of hardware assets that are evaluated using an automated capability that identifies NIST National Vulnerability Database vulnerabilities (CVEs) present with visibility at the organization's enterprise level. CFO Act Agency performance on this metric improved from 81% in FY 2013 to 94% in FY 2014. Fifteen agencies are at or above 95%. As can be seen in **Table 21** the lowest percentages were reported by EPA (74%), DOT (77%), and HHS (77%).

Table 21: Vulnerability Management FY 2013 & FY 2014

Agency	Automated Vulnerability Management FY 2013 (%)	Automated Vulnerability Management FY 2014 (%)
EPA	38	74
DOT	54	77
HHS	84	77
USAID	95	85
HUD	87	86
NRC	95	87
Energy	84	89
Commerce	74	90
VA	63	94
DOD	80	95
OPM	95	95
Treasury	73	97
Labor	96	97
DHS	95	99
Interior	95	99
Justice	99	99
ED	84	100
State	90	100
SSA	94	100
GSA	100	100
NASA	100	100
NSF	100	100
SBA	100	100
USDA	100	100

CFO Act Agency Average*	81	94

*The average is weighted by the total number of the organization's hardware assets connected to the organization's unclassified network(s).

Source: Analysis of FISMA Agency Level Questions Data (Questions 2.1 and 4.1), reported to DHS via CyberScope from October 1, 2012, to September 30, 2014.

Remote Access Authentication

As the Federal Government promotes telework, remote access to network resources requires stronger authentication mechanisms than user ID and password. In order to track agency progress in implementing such measures, agencies are required to report the methods by which users are able to remotely access organizational desktop local area network/wide area network (LAN/WAN) resources. **Table 22** below depicts the percent of users who are required to log on with a two-factor PIV card.

Table 22: Remote Access Authentication FY 2014

Agency	Users required to log onto the organization's remote access solutions with a two-factor PIV Card FY 2014 (%)
ED	0
HUD	0
Labor	0
State	0
EPA	0
NASA	0
NSF	0
NRC	0
SBA	0
USAID	0
Justice	1
DOT	1
VA	3
Energy	9
Commerce	24
USDA	28
DHS	49
Interior	58
HHS	64
Treasury	65
DOD	93
OPM	93
GSA	100
SSA	100
CFO Act Agency Average*	77%

* The average is weighted by the total number of people at the organization who log onto the organization's remote access solution(s) to obtain access to the organization's desktop LAN/WAN resources or services.
Source: Analysis of FISMA Agency Level Questions Data (Questions 5. 10 and 5.11.5) reported to DHS via CyberScope from October 1, 2013, to September 30, 2014.

While the Strong Authentication CAP goal specifically calls for the implementation of PIV-based two factor authentication, the implementation of non-PIV two factor authentication is still a positive cybersecurity measure. To this end, Labor, EPA, NASA, NSF, NRC, SBA, and Justice require 100% of their users to use a non-PIV form of two factor authentication for remote access.

Remote Access Encryption

Remote connections provide opportunities for the compromise of information and require compensating controls to ensure that access is limited to authorized users and connections will not be hijacked. In addition to controls around authentication, agencies also use encryption, malware scans, automated time outs, and other tools to secure remote access.

As part of FISMA reporting, agencies are asked what percentages of their remote access connections have utilized various strategies and technologies to increase remote access security. As illustrated in the following tables, progress implementing these solutions continues but has been, in some cases, uneven. For example, **Table 22** below shows that 18 CFO Act agencies utilize FIPS 140-2 validated cryptographic modules on 100% of remote access connections, but NASA and SBA are at less than 60%.

Table 23: Percentage of remote access connections that utilize FIPS 140-2-validated cryptographic modules

Agency	Remote access connections utilizing FIPS 140-2-validated cryptographic modules FY 2014 (%)
SBA	50
NASA	53
HHS	95
DOD	98
Energy	98
Commerce	99
USDA	100
ED	100
DHS	100
HUD	100
Justice	100
Labor	100
State	100
Interior	100
Treasury	100
DOT	100
VA	100
EPA	100

GSA	100
NSF	100
NRC	100
OPM	100
SSA	100
USAID	100
CFO Act Agency Average	96

Source: Analysis of FISMA Agency Level Questions Data (Question 5.12.1), reported to DHS via CyberScope from October 1, 2013, to September 30, 2014.

Similarly, in **Table 23** below, while 11 agencies prohibit split tunneling and dual connections on 100% of remote access connections, State and USAID do not prohibit split tunneling at all while four other agencies prohibit spilt tunneling for fewer than 40% of remote access connections.

Table 24: Percentage of remote access connections that prohibit split tunneling and/or dual connected remote hosts

Agency	Remote access connections prohibiting split tunneling and/or dual connections FY 2014 (%)
State	0
USAID	0
EPA	15
Energy	17
NRC	29
VA	39
Commerce	71
USDA	79
HHS	80
DHS	92
Labor	92
DOD	97
Treasury	99
ED	100
HUD	100
Justice	100
Interior	100
DOT	100
GSA	100
NASA	100
NSF	100
OPM	100
SBA	100
SSA	100

CFO Act Agency Average	75

Source: Analysis of FISMA Agency Level Questions Data (Question 5.12.2), reported to DHS via CyberScope from October 1, 2013, to September 30, 2014.

Table 24 below illustrates agency performance in accordance with *OMB M-07-16,* *"Safeguarding Against and Responding to the Breach of Personally Identifiable Information,"* which requires that agencies not only implement a time out function for remote access after 30 minutes (or less) of inactivity, but that re-authentication be required to reestablish the session. Again, over half of the CFO Act agencies have 100% of their connections configured with this capability, but three agencies are properly configured for 30% or fewer of their connections.

Table 25: Percentage of remote access connections that are configured to time out after 30 minutes of inactivity

Agency	Remote access connections configured to time-out after 30 minutes of inactivity FY 2014 (%)
USAID	0
OPM	0
DOT	30
NASA	53
HHS	68
DHS	77
USDA	79
Labor	85
DOD	94
Energy	97
Commerce	99
VA	100
Treasury	100
State	100
SSA	100
SBA	100
NSF	100
NRC	100
Justice	100
Interior	100
HUD	100
GSA	100
EPA	100
ED	100
CFO Act Agency Average	83

Source: Analysis of FISMA Agency Level Questions Data (Question 5.12.3), reported to DHS via CyberScope from October 1, 2013, to September 30, 2014.

In the case of remote access connections that scan for malware, **Table 25** below shows that six agencies have configured 100% of their remote access connections with this capability, but 16 agencies report that 50% or fewer of their remote connections have this protection.

Table 26: Percentage of remote access connections that scan for malware upon connection

Agency	Remote access connections that scan for malware upon connection FY 2014 (%)
ED	0
State	0
EPA	0
GSA	0
NSF	0
OPM	0
USDA	4
Energy	8
NASA	11
HHS	18
NRC	29
DOD	30
DHS	31
VA	39
Labor	42
DOT	50
Commerce	62
Treasury	92
HUD	100
Justice	100
Interior	100
SBA	100
SSA	100
USAID	100
CFO Act Agency Average	42

Source: Analysis of FISMA Agency Level Questions Data (Question 5.12.4), reported to DHS via CyberScope from October 1, 2013, to September 30, 2014.

Portable Device Encryption

Mobile devices and unencrypted email are primary sources of loss for sensitive data because they move outside the protection of physical and electronic barriers that protect other hardware assets. Given the risk this presents, the encryption of portable devices was named an Administration priority requiring associated metrics by which to track Federal progress. The ultimate goal is to have 100% of all portable computing devices encrypted with NIST FIPS 140-2[12] validated encryption, which specifies the security requirements for cryptographic modules utilized to protect sensitive but unclassified information, per

OMB Memorandum M-06-16, "Protection of Sensitive Agency Information." [13] **Table 26** below shows that ten agencies are currently at the 100% goal for portable device encryption, but three agencies have fewer than 60% of mobile assets equipped with data encryption.

Table 27: Percentage of mobile assets with encryption of data on the device

Agency	Mobile assets with encryption of data on device FY 2014 (%)
VA	5
NRC	41
Energy	55
NASA	77
USDA	82
DOD	86
Interior	86
SBA	86
EPA	88
HHS	90
Justice	93
Commerce	94
USAID	95
DOT	97
DHS	99
Treasury	99
HUD	100
ED	100
Labor	100
State	100
GSA	100
NSF	100
OPM	100
SSA	100
CFO Act Agency Average*	55

* The average is weighted by the total number of mobile assets at the organization.
Source: Analysis of FISMA Agency Level Questions Data (Questions 6.1.1-6.1.2.5) reported to DHS via CyberScope from October 1, 2013, to September 30, 2014.

Email Encryption

As the Federal Government's reliance on email has increased, so too has the risk of fraudulent emails entering or emanating from Federal agencies. Additionally, unencrypted e-mails are a primary source of sensitive data loss because they move outside the protection of physical and electronic barriers that protect other hardware assets. To combat this threat, agencies provide OMB and DHS with information on the verification (anti-spoofing) and sender verification technologies used to ensure the security of their email systems.

In FY 2014, agencies were asked to report the percentage of agency email systems that both implemented anti-spoofing technologies when sending messages and checked sender verification when receiving messages from outside the network. **Figure 30** below shows that EPA, USAID, and ED have implemented anti-spoofing technologies for sending messages on 0% of email systems, with DOT, Commerce, and HHS implementing on fewer than 70% of systems. EPA and VA have implemented anti-spoofing technologies for receiving messages on 0% of email systems, with DOT and Commerce both implementing on fewer than 70% of systems.

Figure 29: Percentage of Email Systems Implementing Anti-Spoofing Technologies

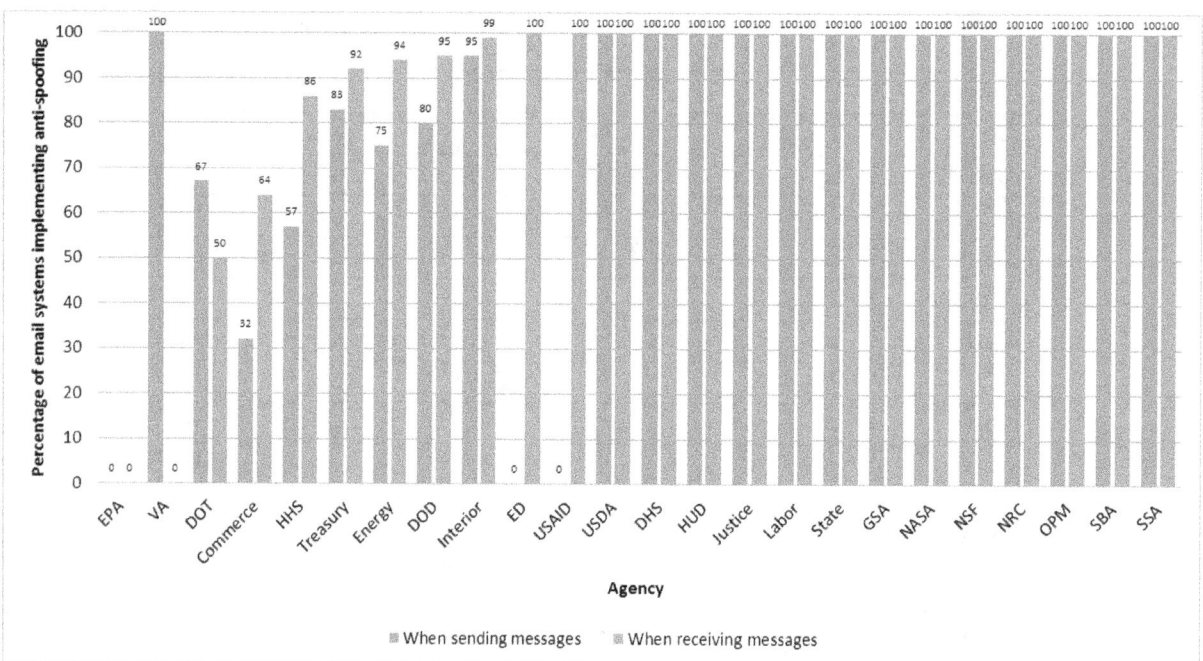

Source: Analysis of FISMA Agency Level Questions Data (Questions 6.2.1 and 6.2.2) reported to DHS via CyberScope from October 1, 2013, to September 30, 2014.

Additionally, **Table 27** below shows that 0% of NASA's email traffic is on systems with the ability to analyze links or attachments in order to identify and quarantine suspected malicious payloads, while DOT and Justice both have less than 75%.

Table 28: Percentage of email systems implementing ability to analyze links or attachments

Agency	Email traffic on systems with the ability to analyze links or attachments FY 2014 (%)
NASA	0
DOT	50
Justice	60
Commerce	78
DOD	84
EPA	90
Interior	95
HHS	96
Energy	97
USDA	100
ED	100
DHS	100
HUD	100
Labor	100
State	100
Treasury	100
VA	100
GSA	100
NSF	100
NRC	100
OPM	100
SBA	100
SSA	100
USAID	100
CFO Act Agency Average	90

Source: Analysis of FISMA Agency Level Questions Data (Questions 6.2.3) reported to DHS via CyberScope from October 1, 2013, to September 30, 2014.

As can be seen in **Table 28** below, SBA, Interior, State, Labor, HUD, and USDA all have no capability to digitally sign email, while EPA, Energy, Commerce, and Treasury have this capability on less than 50% of email systems.

Table 29: Percentage of email systems implementing capability to digitally sign email

Agency	Email traffic on systems implementing capability to digitally sign email FY 2014 (%)
USDA	0
HUD	0
Labor	0
State	0
Interior	0
SBA	0
EPA	1
Energy	13
Commerce	25
Treasury	25
DOT	50
HHS	71
DOD	78
Justice	94
NRC	98
ED	100
DHS	100
VA	100
GSA	100
NASA	100
NSF	100
OPM	100
SSA	100
USAID	100
CFO Act Agency Average	56

Source: Analysis of FISMA Agency Level Questions Data (Questions 6.2.4) reported to DHS via CyberScope from October 1, 2013, to September 30, 2014.

Finally, as can be seen in **Table 29** below, SBA, NSF, DOT State, Labor and USDA have no ability to use FIPS 140-2 Encryption when sending messages, and GSA, EPA, Energy, Treasury, and Commerce have this capability on fewer than 50% of systems. All of this serves to illustrate that, to the extent agencies could improve anti-spoofing technologies as well as the encryption, sigining, and quarantine of emails, their cybersecurity posture could impove as well.

Table 30: Percentage of email systems implementing FIPS 140-2 Encryption of Email

Agency	Email traffic on systems implementing FIPS 140-2 encryption of email FY 2014 (%)
USDA	0
Labor	0
State	0
DOT	0
NSF	0
SBA	0
EPA	1
GSA	1
Energy	11
Treasury	17
Commerce	24
HUD	69
DOD	79
HHS	86
ED	100
DHS	100
Justice	100
Interior	100
VA	100
NASA	100
NRC	100
OPM	100
SSA	100
USAID	100
CFO Act Agency Average	54

Source: Analysis of FISMA Agency Level Questions Data (Questions 6.2.5) reported to DHS via CyberScope from October 1, 2013, to September 30, 2014.

Boundary Protection

Domain Name System Security Extensions (DNSSEC) Implementation

As the Federal Government's reliance on the Internet to disseminate and provide information has increased, one of the risks it has encountered is the potential unauthorized use, compromise, and loss of the .gov domain space. As Domain Name Systems (DNS) translate website names to numeric IP addresses, attackers attempt to hijack the process to take control of the session to, for example, collect user account and password information. The key to defeating such efforts is verifying the integrity of each DNS response received.

DNSSEC provides cryptographic protections to protect against such attacks by digitally 'signing' data so users can be assured it is valid, thereby mitigating the risk of DNS-based attacks and improving the overall integrity and authenticity of information processed over the Internet. The use of DNSSEC was mandated at the Federal level by *OMB Memorandum M-08-23, "Securing the Federal Government's Domain Name System Infrastructure,"* to prevent the pirating of government domain names.[14] GSA has ensured proper DNSSEC for the top level domain names and each organization is responsible for DNSSEC in sub-domain names, which are those below the top-level domain (i.e., www.agency.gov).

NIST developed a monitor to estimate answers to measurement questions about the extent and quality of DNSSEC deployment in the Federal Government and Internet as a whole. **Figure 31** below shows the service information returned by the monitor for the CFO Act agencies on September 30, 2014. The graph shows the number of domains found to be Operational (green), to have some level of DNSSEC configured but not working (In Progress, yellow), and to have no DNSSEC configuration (No Progress, red). DOD and Energy have the highest number of domains with no DNSSEC configuration.

Figure 30: DNSSEC Enabled Domains

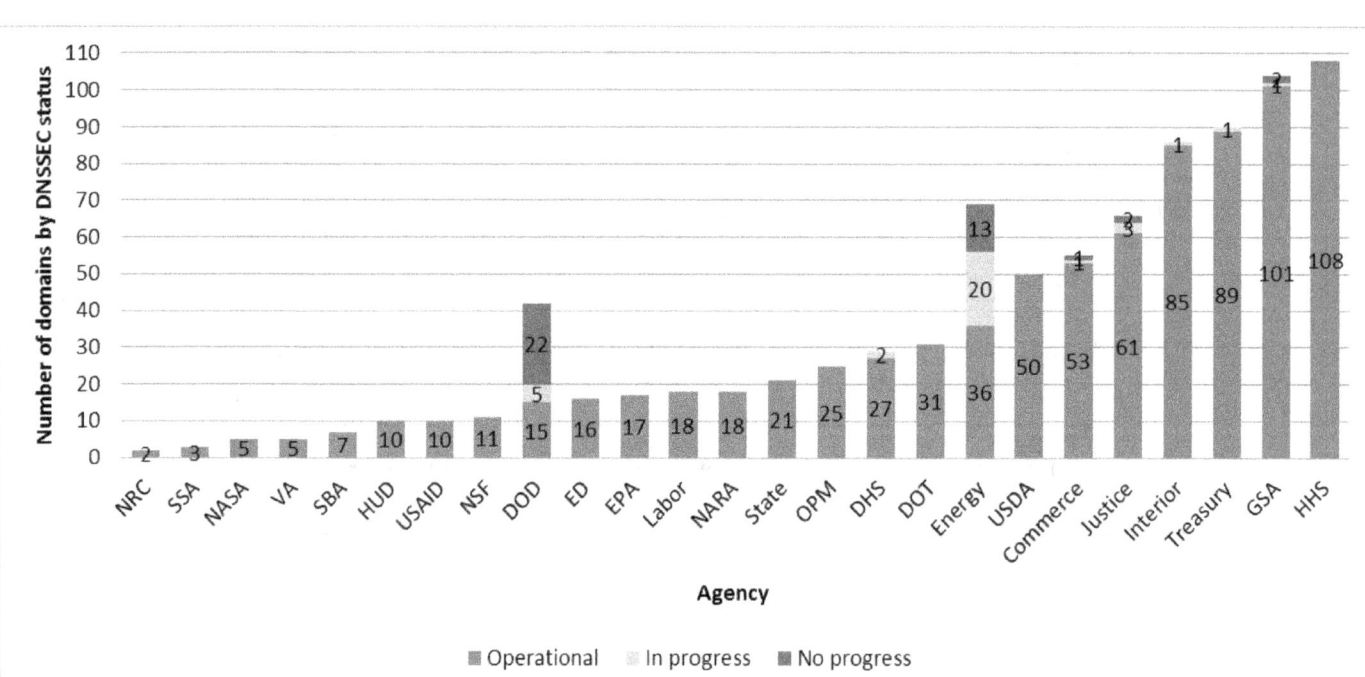

Source: National Institute of Standards and Technology (NIST) data on Estimating DNSSEC External Service Deployment Status on September 30, 2014.

Training and Education

Some of the most effective attacks on cyber-networks are directed at exploiting user behavior. These include phishing attacks, social engineering to obtain passwords, and introduction of malware via removable media. These threats are especially effective when directed at those with elevated network privileges and/or other elevated cyber responsibilities. Training users, both privileged and unprivileged, as well as those with access to other pertinent information and media is a necessary deterrent to these methods. **Figure 32** below shows, by agency, the percentage of network to have completed annual cybersecurity awareness training, as well as the percentage of network users with significant security responsibilities who have taken security training within the organizational standard. Of concern are agencies on the left side of the graph, including NRC, State, USAID, HHS, and DOD, who have less than 75% of users with significant security responsibilities who have taken security training within the organizational standard time.

Figure 31: Security Training

Source: Analysis of FISMA Agency Level Questions Data (Questions 9.1, 9.3, and 9.3.2), reported to DHS via CyberScope from October 1, 2013, to September 30, 2014.

Information Security Metrics for Non-CFO Act Agencies

The non-CFO Act agencies, which consist of small and micro agencies, manage a variety of Federal programs. Their responsibilities include issues concerning commerce and trade, energy and science, transportation, national security, and finance and culture. Approximately one half of all the non-CFO Act agencies perform regulatory or enforcement roles in the Executive Branch. The remaining half is comprised largely of grant-making, advisory, and uniquely chartered organizations. A "small agency" has fewer than six thousand employees; most have fewer than five hundred staff. A "micro agency" has fewer than 100 employees. Together these agencies employ about ninety thousand Federal workers and manage billions of taxpayer dollars.

In FY 2014, 41 small and micro agencies submitted FISMA reports. **Table 30** below contains an aggregated summary of reported performance measures for those agencies that submitted reports. The small agencies responded to the exact same set of metrics in CyberScope the CFO Act agencies, however micro agencies report on a subset of the FISMA metrics.

Table 31: CAP Goal and Key FISMA Metrics (KFMs), Definitions, Sources, and Non-CFO Act Agency Performance FY 2014

Key performance area	Sub-performance area	Definition	Source	Non-CFO Act Agency Performance Average
Information Security Continuous Monitoring (ISCM)	Information Security Continuous Monitoring (ISCM) CAP Goal	The average of automated asset, configuration, and vulnerability management. The average is weighted by the total number of the organization's hardware assets connected to the organization's unclassified network(s).	FISMA Agency Level Questions Data (Questions 2.1, 2.2, and 4.1), and FISMA Agency Level Secure Configuration Management Data on assets reported to DHS via CyberScope from October 1, 2013, to September 30, 2014.	84%
	Automated Asset Management (ISCM) CAP Goal	Percentage of assets where an automated capability (device discovery process) provides visibility at the organization's enterprise level into asset inventory information for all hardware assets. The average is weighted by the total number of the organization's hardware assets connected to the organization's unclassified network(s).	FISMA Agency Level Questions Data (Questions 2.1 and 2.2) reported to DHS via CyberScope from October 1, 2013, to September 30, 2014.	93%
	Automated Asset Management: Detect and Block Unauthorized Software (KFM)	Percentage of applicable assets for which the organization has implemented an automated capability to detect and block unauthorized software from executing or for which no such software exists for the device type. The average is weighted by the total number of the organization's hardware assets connected to the organization's unclassified network(s).	FISMA Agency Level Questions Data (Question 2.1 and 2.5) reported to DHS via CyberScope from October 1, 2013, to September 30, 2014.	45%

Key performance area	Sub-performance area	Definition	Source	Non-CFO Act Agency Performance Average
	Automated Configuration Management (ISCM) CAP Goal	Percentage of the applicable hardware assets of each kind of operating system software that has an automated capability to identify deviations from the approved configuration baselines and provide visibility at the organization's enterprise level. The average is weighted by the total number of the organization's hardware assets connected to the organization's unclassified network(s).	FISMA Agency Level Secure Configuration Management Assets and Percentage Data (Questions 3.1.2 and 3.1.3) reported to DHS via CyberScope from October 1, 2013, to September 30, 2014.	72%
	Automated Vulnerability Management (ISCM) CAP Goal	Percentage of hardware assets that are evaluated using an automated capability that identifies NIST National Vulnerability Database vulnerabilities (CVEs) present with visibility at the organization's enterprise level. The average is weighted by the total number of the organization's hardware assets connected to the organization's unclassified network(s).	FISMA Agency Level Questions Data (Question 2.1 and Question 4.1) reported to DHS via CyberScope from October 1, 2013, to September 30, 2014.	86%
Strong Authentication and Data Protection	Strong Authentication CAP Goal	Percentage of all people required to use Personal Identity Verfication (PIV) to authenticate. The average is weighted by the total number of people at the organization who have network accounts.	FISMA Agency Level Questions Data (Questions 5.1, 5.2.5, 5.3 & 5.4.5) reported to DHS via CyberScope from October 1, 2013, to September 30, 2014.	4%

Key performance area	Sub-performance area	Definition	Source	Non-CFO Act Agency Performance Average
	Remote Access Authentication (KFM)	Percentage of people who are required to log on to the organization's remote access solution(s) to obtain access to the organization's LAN/WAN resources or services using a two-factor PIV card as the nromal mode of authentication for remote access. The average is weighted by the total number of people at the organization who log onto the organization's remote access solution(s) to obtain access to the organization's desktop LAN/WAN resources or services.	FISMA Agency Level Questions Data (Questions 5.10 and 5.11.5) reported to DHS via CyberScope from October 1, 2013, to September 30, 2014.	5%
	Remote Access Encryption: FIPS 140-2 validated cryptographic modules (KFM)	Percentage of remote access connections that utilize FIPS 140-2 validated cryptographic modules.	FISMA Agency Level Questions Data (Question 5.12.1) reported to DHS via CyberScope from October 1, 2013, to September 30, 2014.	73%
	Remote Access Encryption: Prohibits split tunneling (KFM)	Percentage of remote access connections that prohibit split tunneling and/or dual connected remote hosts where the laptop has two active connections.	FISMA Agency Level Questions Data (Question 5.12.2) reported to DHS via CyberScope from October 1, 2013, to September 30, 2014.	66%

Key performance area	Sub-performance area	Definition	Source	Non-CFO Act Agency Performance Average
	Remote Access Encryption: Time-out after 30 minutes of inactivity (KFM)	Percentage of remote access connections that are configured in accordance with OMB M-07-16 to time-out after 30 minutes of inactivity (or less) and require re-authentication to reestablish session.	FISMA Agency Level Questions Data (Question 5.12.3) reported to DHS via CyberScope from October 1, 2013, to September 30, 2014.	72%
	Remote Access Encryption: Scans for malware (KFM)	Percentage of remote access connections that scan for malware upon connection.	FISMA Agency Level Questions Data (Question 5.12.4) reported to DHS via CyberScope from October 1, 2013, to September 30, 2014.	21%
	Data Protection: Mobile Asset Encryption (KFM)	Percentage of mobile assets with encryption of data on the device. The average is weighted by the total number of mobile assets at the organization.	FISMA Agency Level Questions Data (Questions 6.1.1-6.1.2.5) reported to DHS via CyberScope from October 1, 2013, to September 30, 2014.	90%
	Data Protection: Anti-spoofing (KFM)	Percentage of email systems implementing anti-spoofing technologies when sending messages, and when receiving messages.	Sending: FISMA Agency Level Questions Data (Questions 6.2.1) Receiving: FISMA Agency Level Questions Data (Questions 6.2.2) reported to DHS via CyberScope from October 1, 2013, to September 30, 2014.	71% 85%

FEDERAL INFORMATION SECURITY MANAGEMENT ACT

Key performance area	Sub-performance area	Definition	Source	Non-CFO Act Agency Performance Average
	Data Protection: Quarantine maliciouios payload (KFM)	Percentage of email traffic that is on systems that have the capability to analyze llinks or attachmetns to identify and quarantine suspected malicious payload (when receiving messages).	FISMA Agency Level Questions Data (Questions 6.2.3) reported to DHS via CyberScope from October 1, 2013, to September 30, 2014.	90%
	Data Protection: Digitially signed email (KFM)	Percentage of email traffic that is on systems that have the capability to digitially sign email (when sending messages).	FISMA Agency Level Questions Data (Questions 6.2.4) reported to DHS via CyberScope from October 1, 2013, to September 30, 2014.	34%
	Data Protection: Encryption of Email (KFM)	Percentage of email traffic that is on systems that have FIPS 140-2 Encryption of Email (when sending messages).	FISMA Agency Level Questions Data (Questions 6.2.5) reported to DHS via CyberScope from October 1, 2013, to September 30, 2014.	44%
	TIC 2.0 Capabilities CAP Goal	Percentage of the required TIC 2.0 Capabilities implemented.	FISMA Agency Level Questions Data (Questions 7.1) reported to DHS via CyberScope from October 1, 2013, to September 30, 2014.	72%
Boundary Protection	TIC Traffic Consolidation CAP Goal	Percentage of external network traffic to/from the organization's networks that passes through a TIC/MTIPS.	FISMA Agency Level Questions Data (Questions 7.2) reported to DHS via CyberScope from October 1, 2013, to September 30, 2014.	79%

Key performance area	Sub-performance area	Definition	Source	Non-CFO Act Agency Performance Average
	DNSSEC Enabled Domains	Percentage of domains, out of the number tested that were found to be Operational (green), which refers to functional states based on NIST determined characteristics	National Institute of Standards and Technology (NIST) data on Estimating DNSSEC External Service Deployment Status on September 30, 2014.	72%
Training and Education	Security Training (KFM)	Percentage of the organization's network users who were given and successfully completed cybersecurity awareness training in the past year (at least annually). The average is weighted by the total number of people at the organization who have network accounts. & Percentage of the organizations network users and other staff who have significant security responsibilities and have taken security training within the organizational standard for the longest acceptable amount of time between security training events for personnel who have significant security responsibilities. The average is weighted by the total number of network users and other staff at the organization who have significant security responsibilities.	FISMA Agency Level Questions Data (Questions 5.1, 5.3 and 9.1) reported to DHS via CyberScope from October 1, 2013, to September 30, 2014. & FISMA Agency Level Questions Data (Questions 9.3 and 9.3.2 reported to DHS via CyberScope from October 1, 2013, to September 30, 2014.	98% 84%

APPENDIX 4: IT SECURITY SPENDING REPORTED BY CFO ACT AGENCIES

Sufficient resources must be devoted to enable the Federal Government's information and information systems, as well as citizens' information, to remain secure. OMB requires agencies to report information security spending data on an annual basis. All CFO Act agencies reported FY 2014 spending information in the following key areas: Prevent Malicious Cyber Activity; Detect, Analyze, and Mitigate Intrusions; and Shape the Cybersecurity Environment. These areas are explained in greater detail below.

Prevent Malicious Cyber Activity

This area contains categories of spending dedicated to monitoring Federal Government systems and networks and protecting the data within from both external and internal threats. Such categories include:

- TICs;

- Intrusion prevention systems;

- User identity management and authentication;

- Supply chain monitoring;

- Network and data protection;

- Counterintelligence; and

- Insider threat mitigation activities.

Detect, Analyze, and Mitigate Intrusions

This area contains spending on systems and processes used to detect security incidents, analyze the threat, and attempt to mitigate possible vulnerabilities. These categories include:

- CERTs;

- Federal Incident Response Centers;

- Cyber threat analysis;

- Law enforcement;

- Cyber continuity of operations (COOP);

- Incident response and remediation;

- Forensics and damage assessment;

- ISCM and IT security tools; and

- Annual FISMA testing.

Shaping the Cybersecurity Environment

This area contains categories of spending designed to improve the efficacy of current and future information security efforts, including building a strong information security workforce and supporting broader IT security efforts. These categories include:

- NSTIC;

- Workforce development;

- Employee security training;

- Standards development and propagation;

- International cooperation activities; and

- Information security and assurance research and development.

**Table 32: Agency Cybersecurity Spending by Major Category, FY 2014 Actual
(Dollars in Millions)**

Agency	Prevent Malicious Cyber Activity	Detect, Analyze, and Mitigate Intrusions	Shaping the Cybersecurity Environment	Total
Department of Agriculture	$40	$46	$2	$88
Department of Commerce	$56	$83	$74	$213
Department of Education	$11	$20	$1	$32
Department of Energy	$108	$78	$71	$257
Department of Justice	$102	$433	$44	$579
Department of Labor	$13	$3	$1	$17
Department of State	$55	$54	$5	$114
Department of Transportation	$42	$44	$5	$91
Department of Veterans Affairs	$13	$131	$9	$153
Department of the Interior	$17	$30	$1	$48
Department of the Treasury	$122	$68	$10	$200
Department of Defense	$2,552	$1,225	$5,178	$8,955
Department of Health & Human Services	$54	$91	$25	$170
Department of Homeland Security	$473	$722	$148	$1,343
Department of Housing & Urban Development	$6	$8	$0	$14
Environmental Protection Agency	$1	$6	$0	$7
General Services Administration	$27	$16	$10	$53
International Assistance Programs	$9	$4	$3	$16
National Science Foundation	$3	$6	$154	$163
National Aeronautics & Space Administration	$35	$48	$19	$102
Nuclear Regulatory Commission	$4	$12	$3	$19
Office of Personnel Management	$2	$5	$0	$7
Small Business Administration	$1	$4	$0	$5
Social Security Administration	$46	$11	$2	$59
Total Cybersecurity Spending	**$3,792**	**$3,148**	**$5,765**	**$12,705**

NOTE: Due to rounding, categories may not sum to the total

APPENDIX 5: INSPECTORS GENERAL'S RESPONSE

As described in Section III, each agency's Inspector General (IG) was asked to assess his or her department's information security programs in the 11 areas outlined below. Many IGs conducted audits pursuant to generally accepted government auditing standards or inspections pursuant to the Quality Standards for Inspections in order to assess their agencies' cybersecurity programs. All IGs' assessments should include an analysis that consists of two parts: (1) determining if a program was in place for the 11 cybersecurity areas,[15] and (2) evaluating a combined 104 attributes of those programs.[16] The results of these analyses were uploaded into DHS's CyberScope and used to develop this summary. **Table 32** identifies the cybersecurity areas and the respective number of attributes, which are also referred to as the metrics.

Table 33: Attributes by Cybersecurity Area

No.	Cybersecurity Program Area	Attributes
1	Continuous monitoring management	7
2	Configuration management	12
3	Identity and access management	11
4	Incident response and reporting	8
5	Risk management	16
6	Security training	6
7	Plans of action and milestones (POA&M)	8
8	Remote access management	12
9	Contingency planning	12
10	Contractor systems	7
11	Security capital planning	5
	Total	**104**

The following summarizes IG results for (1) CFO Act agencies (2) small and micro agencies, and (3) the 11 cybersecurity areas.[17]

CFO Act Agencies

Table 33 provides the status of CFO Act agencies' programs by cybersecurity area. The assessment scores are based on how many agencies had each of the 11 cybersecurity program areas. The first eight categories provide a percentage based on 24 total CFO Act agencies, however the final three provide percentages based on 23 agencies as one did not report for those metrics.

Table 34: Status of Agency Programs by Cybersecurity Area

	Cyber Security Program Area	Program in place		Program not in place	
		No.	%	No.	%
1	Continuous monitoring	19	79%	5	21%
2	Configuration management	16	67%	8	33%
3	Identity and access management	16	67%	8	33%
4	Incident response and reporting	21	88%	3	13%
5	Risk management	17	71%	7	29%
6	Security training	20	83%	4	17%
7	POA&M	19	79%	5	21%
8	Remote access management	21	88%	3	13%
9	Contingency planning *	17	74%	6	26%
10	Contractor systems *	17	74%	6	26%
11	Security capital planning *	19	83%	4	17%

Source: Data provided to DHS via CyberScope from November 15, 2012, to November 14, 2014.
* One OIG did not report on these programs; therefore, only 23 agencies are included in these areas.

Table 34 provides the CFO Act agencies' cybersecurity assessment scores for fiscal years 2014, 2013 and 2012. The scores are based on (1) whether or not a program was in place for each area, and (2) how many attributes were found in each agency's cybersecurity program. In addition, each cybersecurity area is given equal weight. Within cybersecurity areas, the attributes or metrics are also given equal weight. The table is ordered by FY 2014 scores. Eight agencies scored over 90% (green), which is an increase of 3 from FY 2013, but the same as FY 2012. Eight scored between 65 and 90% (yellow), and the remaining six scored less than 65% (red). Commerce[18] and DOD[19] were not scored.

While the attributes and metrics may have limitations and have been considered by some to be "compliance" oriented, there are several notable observations that can be made. Six agencies (GSA, Justice, DHS, NRC, SSA, and NASA) have consistently performed well when measured against these metrics over the past three years. On the other hand, it is apparent that the CFO Act agencies, as a whole, appear to have stagnant scores that do not reflect significant improvement in addressing these metrics over the last three years. The average score was 76% for fiscal year 2014—the same as in FY 2013. The average for FY 2012 was also 76%.

Table 35: CFO Act Agencies' Scores

Agency	FY 2014 (%)	FY 2013 (%)	FY 2012 (%)
General Services Administration	99	98	99
Department of Justice	99	98	94
Department of Homeland Security	98	99	99
Nuclear Regulatory Commission	96	98	99
Social Security Administration	96	96	98
National Aeronautics and Space Administration	95	91	92
Department of the Interior	92	79	92
Department of Education	91	89	79
National Science Foundation	87	88	90
United States Agency for International Development	86	83	66
Environmental Protection Agency	84	77	77
Department of Labor	82	76	82
Department of Veteran Affair	80	81	81
Department of Energy	78	75	72
Office of Personnel Management	74	83	77
Department of the Treasury	67	76	76
Department of Transportation	63	61	53
Small Business Administration	58	55	57
U.S. Department of Agriculture	53	37	34
Department of State	42	51	53
Department of Health and Human Services	35	43	50
Department of Housing and Urban Development	19	29	66
Department of Defense	N/A*	N/A*	N/A*
Department of Commerce	N/A†	87	61

Source: Data provided to DHS via CyberScope from November 15, 2012, to November 14, 2014.
*Due to the size of the Department, the DOD OIG is unable to definitively report a yes or no answer for all FISMA attributes.
† Commerce OIG's FISMA audit scope was reduced as a result of (1) attrition of several key IT security staff, (2) the need to complete audit work assessing the security posture of key weather satellite systems that support a national critical mission, and (3) additional office priorities. As a result, the FISMA submission primarily focused on assessing policies and procedures, and covered a limited number of systems that would not warrant computation of a compliance score.

For FY 2014, we also assessed the CFO Act agencies' results by type of attribute or metric. DHS designated each attribute or metric as an administrative priority (AP), a key FISMA metric (KFM) or a base metric. **Table 35** compares each agency's overall score with its compliance with (1) APs and (2) APs combined with KFMs. This provides an indication as to how well agencies have addressed the priority and key metrics as compared to their performance over all metrics combined.

Table 36: CFO Act Agencies' Scores (All Attributes, APs, and KFMs) for FY 2014

Agency	FY 2014		
	All Attributes	Administrative Priorities (AP)	AP Plus Key FISMA Metrics
General Services Administration	99	100	89
Department of Justice	99	78	89
Department of Homeland Security	98	100	100
Nuclear Regulatory Commission	96	78	89
Social Security Administration	96	100	94
National Aeronautics and Space Administration	95	100	100
Department of the Interior	92	100	94
Department of Education	91	100	83
National Science Foundation	87	89	83
United States Agency for International Development	86	100	89
Environmental Protection Agency	84	89	89
Department of Labor	82	56	67
Department of Veteran Affairs	80	89	72
Department of Energy	78	22	56
Office of Personnel Management	74	67	78
Department of the Treasury	67	56	44
Department of Transportation	63	22	33
Small Business Administration	58	56	56
U.S. Department of Agriculture	53	44	56
Department of State	42	56	61
Department of Health and Human Services	35	33	44
Department of Housing and Urban Development	19	33	17
Department of Defense	N/A*	N/A*	N/A*
Department of Commerce	N/A†	N/A†	N/A†

Source: Data provided to DHS via CyberScope from November 15, 2012, to November 14, 2014.
* Due to the size of the Department, the DOD OIG is unable to definitively report a yes or no answer for all FISMA attributes.
†Commerce OIG's FISMA audit scope was reduced as a result of (1) attrition of several key IT security staff, (2) the need to complete audit work assessing the security posture of key weather satellite systems that support a national critical mission, and (3) additional office priorities. As a result, the FISMA submission primarily focused on assessing policies and procedures, and covered a limited number of systems that would not warrant computation of a compliance score.

Small and Micro Agencies

The results for the small and micro agencies were comparable to those of the 24 CFO Act agencies. **Table 36** summarizes the results from the IGs of the small and micro agencies according to cyber security program area. These results indicate that the small and micro agencies performed best (i.e., had program programs in place) in security training, incident response and reporting, identity and access management, and remote access management. The weakest performances (i.e., highest number of cases where programs were not in place) occurred in risk management, continuous monitoring management, contingency planning and configuration management.

Table 37: Results for Small and Micro Agencies by Cyber Security Area

Cyber Security Program Area	Program in place		Program not in place	
	FY 2014	%	FY 2014	%
Continuous monitoring	22	58	16	42
Configuration management	25	66	13	34
Identity and access management	29	79	9	24
Incident response and reporting	30	79	8	21
Risk management	22	58	16	42
Security training	31	82	7	18
POA&M	27	71	11	29
Remote access management	29	76	9	24
Contingency planning	24	63	14	37
Contractor systems	26	68	12	32
Security capital planning	28	74	10	26

Source: Data provided to DHS via CyberScope from November 15, 2012, to November 14, 2014.

Table 37 provides the small and micro agencies' assessment scores for FY 2014 and FY 2013. The scoring methodology is the same as the one used for the CFO Act agencies. The table is organized according to agencies' FY 2014 scores. Twelve agencies scored over 90% (green), 12 scored between 65 and 90% compliance (yellow), and the remaining 14 scored less than 65% (red). Four small and micro agencies did not provide data. The average score was 73% for fiscal years 2014, which is comparable to the CFO Act agencies.

Table 38: Micro Agencies' Compliance Scores

Agency	FY 2014 (%)	FY 2013 (%)
Federal Energy Regulatory Commission	100	99
National Transportation Safety Board	100	78
Selective Service System	100	N/A
Overseas Private Investment Corporation	98	84
National Endowment for the Arts	98	N/A
Export-Import Bank of the United States	98	96
Equal Employment Opportunity Commission	95	99
National Credit Union Administration	95	83
Commodity Futures Trading Commission	95	81
Federal Housing Finance Agency	95	95

Millennium Challenge Corporation	94	84
Farm Credit Administration	92	99
Federal Trade Commission	91	92
National Endowment for the Humanities	90	87
Smithsonian Institution	87	88
Federal Reserve Board	87	88
Merit Systems Protection Board	83	88
Tennessee Valley Authority	82	99
Federal Deposit Insurance Corporation	82	87
Consumer Financial Protection Bureau	81	72
Securities and Exchange Commission	77	80
Railroad Retirement Board	73	80
International Boundary and Water Commission	72	53
Federal Labor Relations Authority	70	84
Federal Maritime Commission	66	54
Federal Mediation and Conciliation Service	65	65
Pension Benefit Guaranty Corporation	64	71
National Labor Relations Board	59	87
International Trade Commission	57	51
Corporation for National and Community Service	57	72
Armed Forces Retirement Home	56	N/A
Peace Corps	48	33
Defense Nuclear Facilities Safety Board	47	N/A
Broadcasting Board of Governors	47	50
Court Services and Offender Supervision Agency	39	71
Consumer Product Safety Commission	36	30
Federal Communications Commission	36	N/A
National Archives and Records Administration	16	N/A
Federal Retirement Thrift Investment Board	N/A	N/A
Federal Election Commission	N/A	N/A
Office of Special Counsel	N/A	N/A
Other Defense Civil Programs	N/A	74

Source: Data provided to DHS via CyberScope from November 15, 2012, to November 14, 2014.
NOTE: Federal Retirement Thrift Investment Board, Federal Election Commission, and Office of Special Counsel did not provide the answers with the detail required for scoring for FY 2014. Other Defense Civil Programs did not report answers for FY 2014.

The Eleven Cyber Security Areas

For the 24 CFO Act agencies, the following summarizes the results by the 11 cybersecurity areas.

Information Security Continuous Monitoring

Information security continuous monitoring (ISCM) and adjustment of security controls are essential to protect systems. Security personnel need the real-time security status of their systems, and management needs up-to-date assessments in order to make risk-based decisions. ISCM provides the required real-time view into security control operations, and has become a key focus point for improving Federal information security.

Based on the IGs' reviews, continuous monitoring programs were in place at 19 departments. Seven IGs reported that their department had all components of a continuous monitoring program in place.

The most frequently reported weaknesses or metrics that were not met in continuous monitoring management by the 11 remaining IGs were:

- The department had not implemented ISCM for information technology assets (five departments);

- The department had not evaluated risk assessments used to develop their ISCM strategy (three departments;

- The department had not conducted and reported on ISCM results in accordance with their ISCM strategy (four departments);

- The department had not performed ongoing assessments of security controls (system-specific, hybrid, and common) based on the approved continuous monitoring plans (five departments); and

- The Authorizing Officials and other key system officials with security status were not provided reports covering updates to security plans and security assessment reports, as well as a common and consistent POA&M program that is updated with the frequency defined in the strategy and/or plans (five departments).

Configuration management

To secure both software and hardware, departments must develop and implement standard configuration baselines that prevent or minimize exploitable system vulnerabilities. OMB requires all workstations that use Windows to conform to the U. S. Government Configuration Baseline (USGCB). Furthermore, NIST has created a repository of secure baselines for a wide variety of operating systems and devices.

Based on the IGs' reviews, 16 agencies had configuration management programs in place. However, only three IG reported that his or her department had all of the required attributes of a successful configuration management program. The following deficiencies were most common:

- Assessments of compliance with baseline configurations are not performed (five departments);

- The department does not have a process for timely (as specified in organization policy or standards) remediation of scan result deviations (six departments);

- Windows-based components' USGCB secure configuration settings are were not fully implemented, and any deviations from USGCB baseline settings are not fully documented (seven departments);

- The department does not have a process for timely and secured installation of software patches (four departments);

- Software assessment (scanning) capabilities were not fully implemented (five departments);

- Configuration-related vulnerabilities, including scan findings, had not been remediated in a timely manner (10 departments); and

- Patch management process was not fully developed (five departments).

Identity and access management

Proper identity and access management ensures that users and devices are properly authorized to access information and information systems. Users and devices must be authenticated to ensure that they are who they identify themselves to be. In most systems, a user name and password serve as the primary means of authentication, and the system enforces authorized access rules established by the system administrator. To ensure that only authorized users and devices have access to a system, policy and procedures must be in place for the creation, distribution, maintenance, and eventual termination of accounts. HSPD-12 calls for all Federal departments to require their personnel to use PIV cards. This use of PIV cards is a major component of a secure, government-wide account and identity management system.

Sixteen IGs reported that their departments had identity and access management programs in place. However, not all metrics were met. The most common control weaknesses were:

- The department did not plan for implementation of PIV for logical access (four departments);

- The department did not ensure that the users are granted access based on needs and separation of duties principles (four departments); and

- The department did not ensure that accounts were terminated or deactivated once access was no longer required (seven departments).

Incident response and reporting

Information security incidents occur on a daily basis. Departments must have sound policies and planning in place to respond to these incidents and report them to the appropriate authorities. OMB has designated US-CERT to receive reports of incidents on unclassified Federal Government systems, and requires the reporting of incidents that involve sensitive data, such as personally identifiable information, within strict timelines.

Incident response and reporting programs were largely compliant. Twenty-one IGs reported that their departments had incident response and reporting programs in place. However, 14 IGs identified at least one missing component. The following deficiencies were most common:

- Reports to US-CERT were not made within established timeframes (eight departments);

- The department does not report to law enforcement within established timeframes (three departments);

- The department does not respond to and resolves incidents in a timely manner to minimize further damage (five departments);

- The department is not capable of tracking and managing risks in a virtual/cloud environment (three departments); and

- The department did not respond to and resolve incidents in a timely manner (five departments).

Risk Management

Every information technology system presents risks, and security managers must identify, assess, and mitigate their systems' risks. Federal executives rely on accurate and continuous system assessments since they are ultimately responsible for any risks posed by their systems' operations.

Seventeen IGs reported that their departments had risk management programs in place. However, only four of the 17 reported complete programs, while 13 identified at least one missing component. The following deficiencies were most common:

- The department did not address risk from an organizational perspective with the development of a comprehensive governance structure and organization wide risk management strategy as required by NIST Special Publication 800-37, Revision 1 (six departments);

- The department did not have an up-to-date system inventory (three departments);

- The department did not implement the tailored set of baseline security controls and describe how the controls are employed within the information system and its environment of operation (four departments);

- The department did not assess the security controls using appropriate assessment procedures to determine the extent to which the controls are implemented correctly, operating as intended, and producing the desired outcome with respect to meeting the security requirements for the system (three departments);

- The department did not authorize information system operation based on a determination of the risk to organizational operations and assets, individuals, other organizations, and the nation resulting from the operation of the information system and the decision that this risk is acceptable (three departments); and

- The department did not ensure that information security controls were monitored on an ongoing basis, with assessments of control effectiveness, documentation of system and operation environment changes and security impact analyses of the changes, and reporting on the security state of the system to designated organizational officials (four departments).

Security training

FISMA requires all Federal Government personnel and contractors to complete annual security awareness training that provides instruction on threats to data security and responsibilities in information protection. FISMA also requires specialized training for personnel and contractors with significant security responsibilities. Without adequate security training programs, departments cannot ensure that all personnel receive the required training.

Twenty IGs reported that their departments had compliant programs. Fifteen reported that their departments' programs included all of the required elements. Among the five incomplete programs, the following deficiencies were most common:

- Identification and tracking of the status of security awareness training was not complete for all personnel (employees, contractors, and other organization users) with access privileges that require the training (three departments); and

- Identification and tracking of the status of specialized training was not completed for all personnel with significant information security responsibilities that required specialized training (three departments).

POA&M Remediation

When agencies identify weaknesses in information security systems as the result of controls testing, audits, incidents, continuous monitoring, or other means, it must record each weakness with a POA&M. This plan provides security managers, accreditation officials, and senior officials with information on the overall risk posed to the system by the weaknesses, the actions planned to address the risk, associated costs, and expected completion dates.

Nineteen IGs reported that their departments had POA&Ms in place. Of these 19, eight also indicated that their departments' programs had all of the required attributes. Of the 11 IGs indicating that their programs need improvements, these following issues were most common:

- The department did not track, prioritize and remediate weaknesses (three departments);

- The department did not ensure remediation plans were effective for correcting weaknesses (three departments);

- The department had not established and adhered to milestone remediation dates (seven departments);

- The department did not ensure resources and ownership are provided for correcting weaknesses (three departments); and

- The department did not develop POA&Ms for security weaknesses discovered during assessments of security controls and that require planned mitigation (five departments).

Remote access management

Secure remote access is essential to a department's operations because the proliferation of system access through telework, mobile devices, and information sharing means that information security is no longer confined within system perimeters. Departments also rely on remote access as a critical component of contingency planning and disaster recovery. Each method of remote access requires protections, such as multi-factor authentication, not required for local access.

Twenty-one IGs reported that their departments had remote access management programs in place, and 11 of these had all required attributes. The remaining IGs reported that their departments were missing at least one attribute of a remote access management program. The most common remote access weaknesses were:

- The department lacked documented policies and procedures for authorizing, monitoring, and controlling all methods of remote access (two departments);

- The department did not uniquely identify and authenticate all users for all access (two departments);

- Multi-factor authentication was not required for remote access (four departments); and

- The department did not have a policy to detect and remove unauthorized (rogue) connections (three departments).

Contingency planning

FISMA requires Federal departments to prepare for events that may affect the availability of an information resource. This preparation entails identification of resources and risks to those resources, and the development of a plan to address the consequences if harm occurs. Consideration of risk to a department's mission and the possible magnitude of harm caused by a resource's unavailability are key to contingency planning. Critical systems may require redundant sites that run 24 hours a day, 7 days a week, while less critical systems may not be restored at all after an incident. Once a contingency plan is in place, training and testing must be conducted to ensure that the plan will function in the event of an emergency.

Seventeen IGs reported that their departments had contingency planning programs in place. However, only seven reported that their departments' contingency planning programs were fully compliant with standards. The following issues were prevalent among the 10 departments that needed improvements:

- The department had not performed an overall Business Impact Analysis (four departments);

- The department did not conduct testing of system-specific contingency plans (six departments);

- The department did not have documented BCP and DRP in place for implementing when necessary (six departments); and

- The department did not conduct regular ongoing testing or exercising of business continuity/disaster recovery plans to determine effectiveness and to maintain current plans was performed (five departments).

Contractor Systems

Contractors and other external entities own or operate many information systems on behalf of the Federal Government, including systems that reside in the public cloud. These systems must meet the security requirements for all systems that process or store Federal Government information. Consequently, these systems require oversight by the departments that own or use them to ensure that they meet all applicable requirements.

Seventeen IGs reported that their departments had programs in place to manage contractor systems, but only eight reported that their departments' programs included all required attributes. Nine IGs reported that their departments' programs lacked at least one required element. The most common weaknesses reported were:

- The department did not obtain sufficient assurance that security controls of such systems and services were effectively implemented and complied with Federal and organization guidelines (four departments);

- The department did not have a complete inventory of systems operated on the organization's behalf by contractors or other entities, including organization systems and services residing in a public cloud (three departments); and

- The department had contractor owned or operated systems, some residing in a public cloud, that were not compliant with FISMA requirements, OMB policy, and applicable NIST guidelines (six departments).

Security Capital Planning

Planning for and funding system security must be managed at a department's highest level. Security requirements must be identified, resources estimated, and business cases established to ensure that appropriate levels of security are funded.

Nineteen IGs reported that their departments had security capital planning programs in place. As noted earlier, this section will be removed from DHS's FY 2015 Cybersecurity metrics.

APPENDIX 6: LIST OF CFO ACT AGENCIES

CFO Act Agency	Acronym
Department of Agriculture	USDA
Department of Commerce	Commerce
Department of Defense	DOD
Department of Education	ED
Department of Energy	Energy
Department of Health and Human Services	HHS
Department of Homeland Security	DHS
Department of Housing and Urban Development	HUD
Department of the Interior	Interior
Department of Justice	Justice
Department of Labor	Labor
Department of State	State
Department of Transportation	DOT
Department of the Treasury	Treasury
Department of Veterans Affairs	VA
U.S. Agency for International Development	USAID
Environmental Protection Agency	EPA
General Services Administration	GSA
National Aeronautics and Space Administration	NASA
National Science Foundation	NSF
Nuclear Regulatory Commission	NRC
Office of Personnel Management	OPM
Small Business Administration	SBA
Social Security Administration	SSA

Source: *Chief Financial Officers Act of 1990 (P.L. 101-576)*

APPENDIX 7: LIST OF NON-CFO ACT AGENCIES REPORTING TO CYBERSCOPE

The following agencies submitted FISMA data for this report through CyberScope. CyberScope is a data reporting application developed by DHS and Justice to handle manual and automated inputs of agency data for FISMA compliance reporting.

Non-CFO Act Agency	Acronym
Armed Forces Retirement Home	AFRH
Broadcasting Board of Governors	BBG
Commodity Futures Trading Commission *	CFTC
Consumer Financial Protection Bureau *	CFPB
Consumer Product Safety Commission *	CPSC
Corporation for National and Community Service	CNCS
Court Services and Offender Supervision Agency	CSOSA
Defense Nuclear Facilities Safety Board †	DNFSB
Equal Employment Opportunity Commission	EEOC
Export-Import Bank of the United States	EXIM
Farm Credit Administration †	FCA
Federal Communications Commission	FCC
Federal Deposit Insurance Corporation *	FDIC
Federal Election Commission *	FEC
Federal Energy Regulatory Commission *	FERC
Federal Housing Finance Agency *	FHFA
Federal Labor Relations Authority	FLRA
Federal Maritime Commission	FMC
Federal Mediation and Conciliation Service	FMCS
Federal Reserve Board *	FRB
Federal Retirement Thrift Investment Board †	FRTIB
Federal Trade Commission *	FTC
International Boundary and Water Commission	IBWC
International Trade Commission	USITC
Merit Systems Protection Board	MSPB
Millennium Challenge Corporation	MCC
National Archives and Records Administration	NARA
National Credit Union Administration	NCUA
National Endowment for the Arts	NEA
National Endowment for the Humanities	NEH
National Labor Relations Board *	NLRB
National Transportation Safety Board	NTSB
Office of Special Counsel	OSC
Other Defense Civil Programs	ODCP
Overseas Private Investment Corporation	OPIC

Non-CFO Act Agency	Acronym
Peace Corps	PC
Pension Benefit Guaranty Corporation	PBGC
Railroad Retirement Board	RRB
Securities and Exchange Commission *	SEC
Selective Service System	SSS
Smithsonian Institution	SI
Tennessee Valley Authority	TVA

* Independent Regulatory Agency (44 USC 3502(5))
† Micro Agency

END NOTES

[1] As described in *OMB Memorandum M-14-08, Fiscal Year 2014 PortfolioStat*, PortfolioStat is "a data-driven review of agency portfolio management with the Federal Chief Information Officer (CIO), the agency Deputy Secretary, agency CIOs, and other senior agency officials."

[2] As described in OMB Memorandum M-15-01, CyberStat reviews are face-to-face, evidence-based meetings to ensure agencies are accountable for their cybersecurity posture, while at the same time assisting them in developing focused strategies for improving their information security posture.

[3] FY 2014 funding was provided by the *Consolidated Appropriations Act, 2014* (Pub. L. No. 113-76); FY 2015 funding was provided by the *Consolidated and Further Continuing Appropriations Act, 2015* (Pub. L. No. 113-235).

[4] A computer security incident, as defined by NIST SP 800-61, "Computer Security Incident Handling Guide," is a violation or imminent threat of violation of computer security policies, acceptable use policies, or standard computer security practices.

[5] Progress Update, FY 2014, Quarter 4, Cybersecurity Cross Agency Priority Goal, *http://www.performance.gov/node/3401/view?view=public#progress-update*

[6] Due to its large number of users, DOD's Strong Authentication implementation percentage inflates the government-wide implementation percentage. Including DOD, 54% of Federal civilian cybersecurity incidents in FY 2014 were related to or could have been prevented by Strong Authentication. In FY 2013, this number was 66%.

[7] DOD is excluded from the visualization because it would obscure the data due to its large number of users. DOD reports that 3,174,838 of its unprivileged network users are required to use two-factor PIV card authentication compared to 396,855 users who are able to log on with user ID and password alone.

[8] DOD is excluded from the visualization because it would obscure the data due to its large number of users. DOD reports that 26,684 of its privileged network users are required to use two-factor PIV card authentication compared to 34,408 users who are able to log on with user ID and password alone.

[9] DHS, pursuant to the authority provided by OMB, issued the *FY 2014 Inspector General FISMA Reporting Metrics* on December 2, 2013. This document includes general instructions as well as the 104 attributes.

[10] Commerce OIG's FISMA audit scope was reduced as a result of (1) attrition of several key IT security staff, (2) the need to complete audit work assessing the security posture of key weather satellite systems that support a national critical mission, and (3) additional office priorities. As a result, the FISMA submission primarily focused on assessing policies and procedures, and covered a limited number of systems that would not warrant computation of a compliance score.

[11] Due to the size of the Department, the DOD OIG is unable to definitively report a yes or no answer for all FISMA attributes.

[12] NIST FIPS 140-2, "Security Requirements for Cryptographic Modules," is available at:

http://csrc.nist.gov/publications/fips/fips140-2/fips1402.pdf

[13] OMB Memorandum M-06-16, "Protection of Sensitive Agency Information," (June 23, 2006), available at: _www.WhiteHouse.gov/sites/default/files/omb/memoranda/fy2006/m06-16.pdf_

[14] OMB Memorandum M-08-23, " Securing the Federal Government's Domain Name System Infrastructure," (August 22, 2008), available at: _www.WhiteHouse.gov/sites/default/files/omb/assets/omb/memoranda/fy2008/m08-23.pdf_

[15] In FY 2015, Security Capital Planning will no longer be considered a cybersecurity area for purposes of populating Cyberscope, leaving 10 program areas.

[16] DHS, pursuant to the authority provided by OMB, issued the FY 2014 Inspector General FISMA Reporting Metrics on December 2, 2013. This document includes general instructions as well as the 104 attributes.

[17] The results for the eleven cybersecurity areas are based on the CFO Act agencies only.

[18] Commerce OIG's FISMA audit scope was reduced as a result of (1) attrition of several key IT security staff, (2) the need to complete audit work assessing the security posture of key weather satellite systems that support a national critical mission, and (3) additional office priorities. As a result, the FISMA submission primarily focused on assessing policies and procedures, and covered a limited number of systems that would not warrant computation of a compliance score.

[19] Due to the size of the Department, the DOD OIG is unable to definitively report a yes or no answer for all FISMA attributes.